CH
DE

CHILD
DEVELOPMENT

NT

ook

book

Jacqueline Harding

HODDER
EDUCATION
AN HACHETTE UK COMPANY

Orders: please contact Bookpoint Ltd, 130 Milton Park, Abingdon, Oxon OX14 4SB. Telephone: (44) 01235 827720. Fax: (44) 01235 400454. Lines are open from 9.00–5.00, Monday to Saturday, with a 24 hour message answering service. You can also order through our website www.hoddereducation.co.uk.

British Library Cataloguing in Publication Data

A catalogue record for this title is available from the British Library

ISBN: 9781444183818

First Published 2013

Impression number 10 9 8 7 6 5 4 3 2 1

Year   2016 2015 2014 2013

Hachette UK's policy is to use papers that are natural, renewable and recyclable products and made from wood grown in sustainable forests. The logging and manufacturing processes are expected to conform to the environmental regulations of the country of origin.

Cover photo © Hodder Education

Typeset by Datapage (India) Pvt. Ltd.

Printed in Italy for Hodder Education, an Hachette UK company, 338 Euston Road, London NW1 3BH

CONTENTS

ACKNOWLEDGEMENTS

Firstly, I wish to thank the children and parents for their kind permission to film and photograph their children in order that we should all learn more about how children develop. We hope you had fun too!

Huge thanks to Rachel Burrell for her unending patience when taking photographs and capturing the very skill needed; Sam Harding for his aptitude and excellence in filming each child's development with the care and precision that are needed; and Holly-Anne Harding for her dedicated contribution to the writing of the book. Debbie Green, you are a rock. Tomorrow's Child team – I am so proud of you all.

Thanks to Alan Holloway for his remarkable expertise in Photoshop.

Also, huge gratitude to Kym Scott for her expertise and knowledge in the early years of life and her generosity of time spent ensuring that the information is accurate (what a wonderful 'find' you are). Di, you are a star – thank you so much for helping to make sure that 'every child' is represented in this book; and head teacher Celia Dawson, for her thoughts on inclusion.

Power Parenting team, your support has been invaluable.

Big thanks to Colin Goodlad, Stephen Halder, Chloé Harmsworth and Gemma Parsons at Hodder for excellent guidance and expertise at getting this book to work.

Thanks also to the practitioners and students who reviewed the book and took the time to explain the parts that were difficult to understand.

PS Big thanks to all my friends and family for understanding when, yet again, I had to cancel to write this book. Chris and George – accountants extraordinaires – thank you!

And, Ian Richards, a 'shout out' for your support and the 'countdown'!

FOREWORD

Jacqueline's never-ending energy and enthusiasm for truly understanding children are demonstrated in this book. As a medical doctor, I am impressed by her plea to understand that development is holistic and that we must all strive to understand each child and their individual potential.

Dr Sanjay Chaudhuri, MBBS, BSc

Parents have a keen interest in child development matters, and they often turn to the health professionals they're meeting on a regular basis, looking for answers to their questions. This great book is the one that those professionals should turn to when they want to have the right information at their fingertips. Written in a down-to-earth, practical, easily accessible style, with the added value of informative film clips and wonderful photography, this book is a must-have for everyone working with young children.

It is light years away from the old-fashioned child development textbooks that were probably a heavy read for many working with young children. It uses simple language and clear key points, with each section helpfully divided into physical development, personal, social, emotional development, intellectual development, and communication and language. Each chapter is visually led for the way people prefer to receive information in the modern world, and, moreover, it does this for every stage right through childhood from birth to age 19.

Eileen Hayes, MBE, Parenting Consultant

ABOUT THE AUTHOR

Jacqueline Harding, Director of Tomorrow's Child

Jacqueline is internationally known as a leading child development expert and she has extensive experience of advising programme makers, web and interactive media designers about how to match content to the needs of the developing child.

She has written books on child development, observing children and the value of play (and books for children, too). Her company has made hundreds of films about children, youth and families and also produces content for children. She is director of Tomorrow's Child and Parentchannel.tv.

About Tomorrow's Child

Tomorrow's Child UK Ltd is a unique research and media company that specialises in children, youth and families. Tomorrow's Child works with clients from across Europe to ensure that their media proposition for children is developmentally correct, engages the young developing brain in the best way possible and offers an active experience.

www.tomorrowschild.co.uk

Parentchannel.tv

In 2008, Jacqueline had the vision for an online video resource for parents and set about producing a pilot. In 2010, **www.parentchannel** was successfully launched with two hundred films and is helping thousands of parents. Parenting UK works in collaboration with Tomorrow's Child on parenting projects.

INTRODUCTION

What is so special about child development and why should this area be studied?

Children are endlessly fascinating. Studying their development is one of the most enlightening experiences for anyone. For students and practitioners, it is essential. Without an understanding of how children develop, we fail to acknowledge one of the most important pieces of the jigsaw puzzle when providing for them.

Is it possible to know everything about child development? No, it's just not achievable. Every child is unique. Babies, children and young people will continue to surprise us for as long as we work with them. And, as new research emerges, especially into the developing brain, we will continue to be amazed at their developing skills and abilities.

This book has been written with a focus on explaining child development as clearly and as visually led as possible. A variety of methods has been used, for example video, photographs and enlarged images; all supplemented by everyday language, bullet-pointed within the text.

With a keen eye for keeping the delight of the developing child at the centre, the book has been formatted in a way that hopes to keep it 'real and relevant' for both student and practitioner.

Who is this book suitable for?

This book has been written for readers who are keen to understand more about child development in a way that presents the information mostly in a visual way.

Students, practitioners and parents are busy people. Students on any professional course relating to children and young people, through to practitioners of any level of experience, will be able to make good use of the information straight away.

This book is also a great way to get up to date with new research into child development. In order to keep the developmental theory 'real', simple and cost-effective activities are suggested. The aim is to demonstrate the developing skills and abilities clearly in an easy-to-absorb format so that quite quickly it will help equip the student or practitioner to translate their knowledge into suitable activities.

Each activity relates to development and has a variety of aims, for example to encourage the child's development further and to identify or pinpoint any difficulties as soon as possible. Early intervention makes a difference. The sooner a child's challenges are noted, the sooner appropriate action can be taken.

Leading UK awarding bodies in child care and education, such as CACHE (Council for Awards in Care, Health and Education), City and Guilds and Edexcel (BTEC), define particular areas of development, and for ease of understanding this book follows the definitions provided.

Children's rights

The United Nations Convention on the Rights of the Child 1989 makes it clear that children are entitled to provision which enables them to develop their personalities, talents and abilities irrespective of ethnicity, culture or religion, home language, family background, learning difficulties, disabilities or gender.

An in-depth knowledge of how children develop is the best starting point to ensure these entitlements become a reality.

Inclusion

Too often, matters relating to inclusion are relegated to the back of a book. The author believes that any aspect of inclusion should be considered mainstream, therefore all comments regarding children with special educational needs and disabilities are included within the main text. The term 'special educational needs' has a legal definition. The term refers to children who have learning difficulties or disabilities that make it harder for them to learn or access education than most children of the same age. It is important that their individual needs be met and they receive a broad, well-balanced and relevant education.

Families with young disabled children often say that they want to be treated as a family and a child, not as a medical case. The photographs and films of children with additional needs and disabilities in this book are demonstrations of what the particular child photographed or filmed could achieve.

Practitioners need a clear understanding of the needs of all children in their care: including those with additional educational needs, those of high ability, those with English as an additional language and those with additional disabilities. Using the correct approach to engage and support all children is the responsibility of the practitioner.

Child development and child care qualifications

This book addresses the areas of development included in a number of qualifications provided by leading UK awarding bodies. Listed below are some of the main qualifications and units that the content of this book will help to support.

CACHE Level 2 Child Care and Education Award/ Certificate/Diploma

The content of this book is mainly relevant to **Unit 2 The developing child**, but also helps to support elements of other units in the CACHE Level 2 Child Care and Education Award/Certificate/Diploma, including:

➤ Unit 3 Safe, healthy and nurturing environments for children
➤ Unit 4 Children and play
➤ Unit 7 Working with children from birth to age 5 years
➤ Unit 9 Supporting children with additional needs
➤ Unit 10 Introduction to children's learning

CACHE Level 3 Child Care and Education Award/Certificate/Diploma

The content of this book is mainly relevant to **Unit 2 Development from conception to age 16 years**, but may also help to support the following units of CACHE Level 3 Child Care and Education Award/Certificate/Diploma:

➤ Unit 3 Supporting children
➤ Unit 14 Working with children with special needs
➤ Unit 15 Developing children's (3–8 years) mathematical skills
➤ Unit 16 Developing children's (3–8 years) communication, language and literacy skills
➤ Unit 18 Working with babies from birth to 12 months

This book also covers **every theory of development as directed by CACHE**:

1 Nature versus nurture
2 Piaget's theory of cognitive development
3 Vygotsky's studies of the way children learn
4 Chomsky's, Skinner's and Vygotsky's views of language development
5 Theories of social and emotional development attachment, separation and loss (Bowlby, James and Joyce Robertson)
6 Skinner – implications for behaviour management
7 Current theorists – such as Margaret Donaldson, Cathy Nutbrown, the Effective Provision of Pre-School Education (EPPE), Chris Athey and Tina Bruce
8 Factors that affect development

Children and Young People's Workforce (CYPW)

This book also covers the development of the age range from birth to nineteen years, as required for the CYPW qualification. It includes information that will be useful to those studying the following units:

Level 2 Certificate Children and Young People's Workforce

➤ Child and young person development
➤ Contribute to the support of child and young person development
➤ Support children and young people with disabilities and special educational needs

➤ Contribute to the support of children's communication, language and literacy
➤ Contribute to the support of children's creative development

Level 3 Diploma Children and Young People's Workforce

➤ Understand child and young person development
➤ Promote child and young person development
➤ Promote learning and development in the early years
➤ Support children's speech, language and communication
➤ Work with babies and young children to promote their development and learning
➤ Promote young children's physical activity and movement skills
➤ Support disabled children and young people and those with specific requirements

BTEC

The content of this book is also relevant to BTEC Level 2 First Children's Play, Learning and Development and BTEC Level 3 National Children's Play, Learning and Development. You will find information that may be useful for the following units:

BTEC First Children's Play, Learning and Development

➤ Unit 1 Patterns of child development
➤ Unit 2 Promoting children's development through play

BTEC National Children's Play, Learning and Development

➤ Unit 1 Child development
➤ Unit 2 Play in Early Years Settings
➤ Unit 6 Supporting Children's Communication and Language
➤ Unit 7 Supporting Children's Personal, Social and Emotional Development
➤ Unit 15 Working with Children Under Three Years
➤ Unit 18 Working With Children With Additional Needs
➤ Unit 19 Promoting Mathematical Development in Children Aged from Four up to Eight Years
➤ Unit 20 Promoting Literacy in Children Aged from Four up to Eight Years
➤ Unit 22 Implementing the Early Years Foundation Stage in England
➤ Unit 26 Supporting Children's Creativity

➤ Unit 28 Promoting Children's Development Outdoors
➤ Unit 32 Meeting the Needs of Children Who May Have an Autism Spectrum Disorder

National Occupational Standards

The National Occupational Standards in Children's Care, Learning and Development require that children's development is studied from birth to sixteen. This book continues to nineteen years, to cover the requirements of the CYPW qualification, and as we believe it's important to have a clear knowledge of child development to adulthood.

The progress check at age two

This 'progress check' is referred to on the appropriate pages for two-year-olds and the developmental points provided on the pages leading up to the check should prove to be an invaluable resource.

The aims of the progress check at age two are to:

➤ review a child's development in the three prime areas of the EYFS;
➤ ensure that parents have a clear picture of their child's development;
➤ enable practitioners to understand the child's needs and plan activities to meet them in the setting;
➤ enable parents to understand the child's needs and, with support from practitioners, enhance development at home;
➤ note areas where a child is progressing well and identify any areas where progress is less than expected; and
➤ describe actions the provider intends to take to address any developmental concerns (including working with other professionals where appropriate).

Of course, student and practitioners should also refer to the EYFS Development Matters materials for guidance.

HOW TO USE THIS BOOK

Points about development

For each age range, there are short notes about key developmental points to provide an at-a-glance overview. It is not intended to be an exhaustive list as some skills are demonstrated in the films or photographs provided. Some skills have not been noted. For in-depth notes please see References and further reading, page 173.

Three prime areas

The EYFS has been subjected to review and it is now simpler, with an emphasis on the three prime areas: communication and language; physical; and personal, social and emotional development. It was implemented in September 2012.

In this book, examples are provided to show how children at each stage of development can make their way towards those goals.

EYFS

Explains the subject's relevance to the EYFS.

Key debate

Developmental theory and topical issues explained.

Activity

Examples of activities to try.

Inclusion point

This area will include aspects of inclusion.

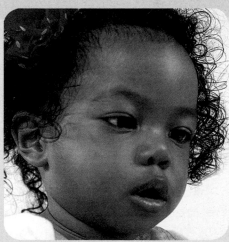

Photographs are included to show the development stage being discussed. Some sections of the photos are enlarged to give you a clearer view.

Captions in blue: give information needed for Level 2 students.

Captions in purple: give slightly greater depth for Level 3 students.

Using the QR codes

To use the QR codes you will need a QR code reader for your smartphone/tablet. There are many free QR code readers available dependent on the smartphone/tablet you are using. We have supplied some suggestions below of well-known QR readers, but this is not an exhaustive list and you should only download software compatible with your device and operating system. We do not endorse any of the third-party products listed below and downloading them is at your own risk:

iphone/ipad – Qrafter – **http://itunes.apple.com/app/qrafter-qr-code-reader-generator/id416098700**

Android – QR Droid – **https://market.android.com/details?id=la.droid.qr&hl=en**

Blackberry – QR Scanner Pro – **http://appworld.blackberry.com/webstore/content/13962**

Windows/Symbian – Upcode – **http://www.upc.fi/en/upcode/download/**

Once you have downloaded a QR code reader, simply open the reader app and use it to take a photo of the code. The resource will then load on your smartphone/tablet.

Via the website

If you do not have a smartphone/tablet, you can view any of these videos online by visiting the website http://www.hodderplus.co.uk/childdevelopment/. The resources are listed by chapter.

We are interested in your feedback on the QR codes included with this title. If you have any comments, please send them to educationenquiries@hodder.co.uk.

AREAS OF DEVELOPMENT EXPLAINED

What does child development really mean?

Although areas of development are often described separately, mostly for ease of explanation, it is important to keep in mind that the developing child must be seen as a whole.

The sentences used to describe the age ranges at the beginning of each chapter have been carefully chosen to reflect this view. Children usually start to demonstrate a skill 'around or approaching' a particular age, rarely on the date of their next birthday. The development demonstrated in each chapter describes a typical range of development within that age bracket.

Adopting a rigid approach to understanding development is unhelpful. Checklists are a poor approach to adopt. At the same time, milestones are important benchmarks. Having a visual model, as provided by the films and photographs, can be an effective way to recall developmental skills. A picture in the mind can act as a suitable reference on which to build other reference points. For example, another child may master a skill or develop in an unexpected way. That 'picture' can be added to the repertoire of how different children achieve skills in a variety of ways.

Making a difference as soon as possible

Practitioners equipped with the knowledge of how children develop are often the first to be aware of a child who appears to be encountering developmental difficulties.

The parent/carer is often also aware and may raise a concern too. Equally, a parent/carer may be unaware of a difficulty and the keen observation of the practitioner can be crucial in getting the support needed at an early stage.

Early intervention works. Children benefit from intervention that swiftly addresses a difficulty in the right way, and carefully planned activities will support them and can make a positive difference in a short time.

Developmental theories are interesting to read and more importantly to learn to apply in the workplace. The actual application of the theory to practice is what truly counts.

It's always a good idea to take a broad view. Observations of a child in various situations at differing times and with varying developmental focus can reveal

more than first might be thought. Recording notes and taking a considered approach can lead to a more accurate picture of where the child is developmentally at any given point. Equipped with sufficient information, decisions that truly benefit the child can be taken in discussion with other professionals and parents/carers.

Factors affecting development

There are many reasons that can help or hinder growth and development. Identified below are a few of the main factors that can be positive or negative:

- quality of parental relationship with child and support given at home (DFE-funded research such as Charles Desforges and EPPE found that this was the most important factor, even when all the factors below were taken into account, i.e. all of those below can be overcome if the parent is willing and able to support their child's learning and development in a positive home-learning environment)
- opportunities for parents to work
- opportunities for children to acquire education
- income
- housing
- environmental factors (safe or unsafe)
- disruption or stability (within family structures/relationships and environment, e.g. housing and financial incomes)
- health status
- gender (boys and girls differ in their rates of growth)
- genetics (inherited factors).

It is important to take into account any potential factors when an overall assessment or profile of a particular child's development is to be made.

Equality of opportunity and anti-discriminatory practice

These two important areas of practice ensure that every child is included and supported. It is a priority that students and practitioners understand the Equal Opportunity and Anti-Discriminatory policies at their work or work placement.

Safeguarding and welfare requirements

The Safeguarding and Welfare Requirements set standards to help early years providers meet the needs of children. Section 3.1 states:

> *'Children learn best when they are healthy, safe and secure, when their individual needs are met and when they have positive relationships with the adults caring for them. The safeguarding and welfare requirements, specified in this section, are designed to help providers create high-quality settings which are welcoming, safe and stimulating, and where children are able to enjoy learning and grow in confidence.'*

Students and practitioners need to understand the safeguarding policy at their work or work placement.

Confidence as a practitioner

Confidence as a practitioner takes time. Try taking this book around with you while observing children in your care. Observing children's development in varying situations and across the ages from birth to 19 eventually results in a valuable overview of development.

Studying child development through to 19 years is essential. It helps put the pieces of the puzzle together. Then observing children in other settings in different situations broadens your knowledge even further. Recording your observation and thoughts, sharing them with those more experienced in the workplace, or with college lecturers, can lead to a valuable insight into how children learn.

The ability to respond in the right way and at the right time builds a practitioner's confidence and can reap a critical reward for the developing child.

Areas of development

Two important points:

1 Every child is unique.
2 Children develop at their own rates, and in their own ways.

Below is a useful description of each area of development that you will find throughout this book.

Personal, social and emotional

This area is about the:

➤ development of a positive sense of self and others
➤ formation of positive relationships
➤ development of respect for others
➤ development of social skills
➤ management of feelings
➤ understanding of appropriate behaviour in groups
➤ confidence in own abilities.

Physical development

This area is about the:

➤ development of coordination control and movement
➤ gross motor skills – these concern movements made by arms, legs, or entire body. These skills involve the large muscles of the body that enable, for example, walking and kicking to develop
➤ fine motor skills – these concern the small movements of the body and use the muscles that enable, for example, grasping small objects and fastening buttons.

Communication and language

This area is about the:

➤ development of language
➤ development of confidence and skills in expression
➤ ability to speak and listen in a range of situations.

Intellectual

This area is about the:

➤ development of understanding, analysis and evaluation of concepts and the ability to make sense of the world.

Why are people and the environment so important?

'Children develop in the context of relationships and the environment around them. This is unique to each family, and reflects individual communities and cultures.'

(Development Matters in the Early Years Foundation Stage, Department for Education, 2012)

This means that people around the baby and child are important in terms of how they relate to them, and the environment is important in terms of how the baby or child is encouraged to interact with it.

What are the characteristics of effective learning?

These three areas are helpful when you are thinking about activities to support a child's development.

1. Playing and exploring:

➤ Finding out and exploring
➤ Playing with what they know
➤ Being willing to 'have a go'

2. Active learning:

➤ Being involved and concentrating
➤ Keeping trying
➤ Enjoying and achieving what they set out to do

3. Creating and thinking critically:

➤ Having their own ideas
➤ Making links
➤ Choosing ways to do things

Active play

Young children love to be creative. Allowing them to explore the world will help develop their intellectual, physical, and emotional skills.

2 BIRTH AND THE FIRST MONTH

Video

Scan the QR code opposite to view a video demonstrating development for birth and the first month.
You can also access this video at http://tinyurl.com/al4p5pp

Physical development

Key debate

Dr John Bowlby, researching from the 1950s to 1970s, thought that early attachment was very important. His work led to changes in the treatment of children in hospitals. The way in which young babies experience relationships influences all future relationships (Perry, 1995; Karr-Morse and Wiley, 1997).

Piaget's (1896–1980) sensori-motor period (birth to two years) outlines the early stages between birth and one month as the time for reflex activity – that is, turning towards sound, eye movements, grasping and sucking.

Recent advances in brain research show how brain cells increase at a far greater pace between birth and one year than at any other time. These findings highlight the importance of the primary or main carer, who has the greatest impact on this (Schore, 2000).

Discuss how important you think consistent contact with parents/carers is to a young baby.

Reflexes

At birth, the baby is already equipped to use their senses to begin to make sense of the world. Reflexes are automatic responses to a stimulus, for example, touch.

Activity

When a baby is alert and perhaps spending time on their tummy, try different tones of gentle music for baby and note how they respond. Try 'conversation play' with baby by taking turns singing to them and then waiting for a response. Even if there is little response at first – press on, it will be worth it – baby is learning the art of future conversation making!

Inclusion point

Babies with hearing loss will make similar vocalisations at this stage but may not show the startle reflex in response to a loud sound.

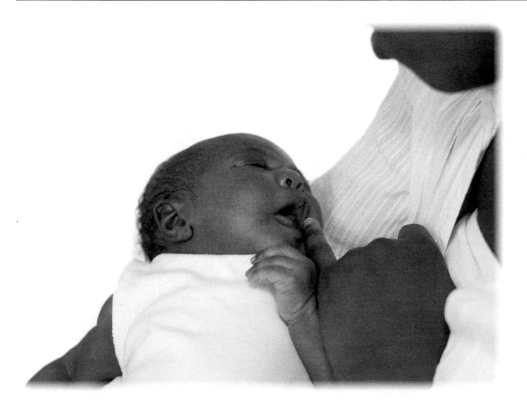

Rooting reflex

Level 2: As her cheek is stroked, she will turn towards that side as if to seek a nipple with her mouth.

Level 3: Rooting fades at about four months.

Grasp reflex (palmer grasp)

Level 2: She will grasp any object placed in the palm of her hand.

Level 3: The grasp reflex fades at about four months.

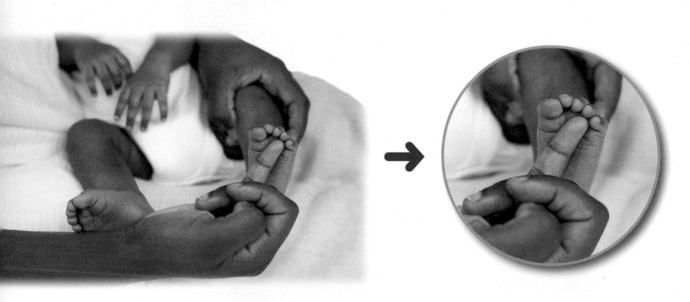

Toe grasp (plantar grasp)

Level 2: She will curl her toes when the sides of her foot are gently pressed.

Level 3: Babinski's sign: her big toe curls and other toes fan out when the side of her foot is stroked. This fades at around 12 months.

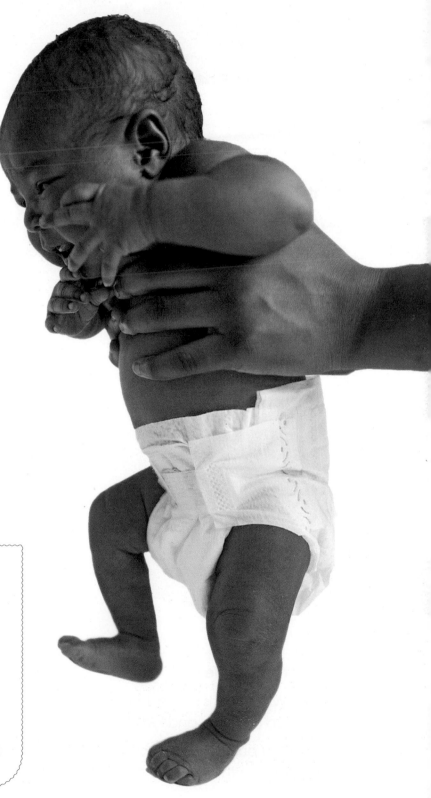

Stepping reflex

Level 2: When she is held upright (with the soles of her feet on a flat surface) she will make a stepping movement.

Level 3: This stepping reflex will disappear by three or four months and becomes a voluntary behaviour at around 8-12 months.

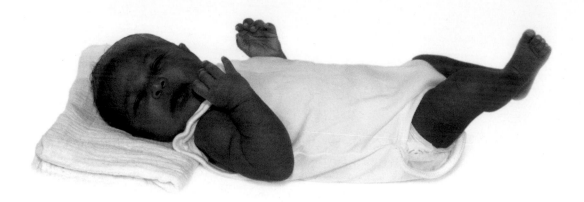

Blinking eyes

Level 2: Her eyelids will close and open again to sudden visual stimulus.

Level 3: Blinking is a reflex that carries on throughout life to protect and moisten the eyeball.

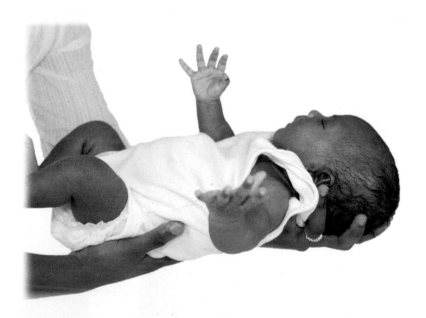

Moro startle reflex

Level 2: When she is startled, her arms and legs will open and she will arch her back. Then her arms and legs close.

Level 3: The purpose of the closure part with arms and legs appears to be to hang onto another human to avoid falling.

Gross motor skills

He/she:

➤ can turn their head to one side when lying on their back
➤ can turn over from side to back
➤ can lift their head very briefly from the prone position
➤ makes uncontrollable arm and leg movements.

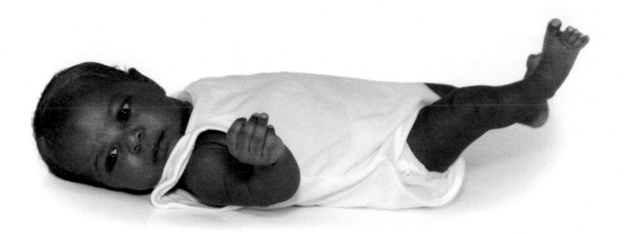

Head to one side

Level 2: She lies with her head to one side while on her back.

Level 3: This is called the supine position.

Pulled to sitting

Level 2: She cannot control her neck muscles and her head will lag behind when pulled to sitting position without essential support.

Level 3: Her back is curved and head lags and requires essential support.

Fine motor skills

He/she:

➤ will have their hands closed but may open them when the back of their hand is stroked.

Fist to mouth

Level 2: She can bring her fist to her mouth.

Level 3: She will suck rhythmically objects placed in her mouth. Rhythmic sucking fades around six months, although babies, children and adults can suck at will.

Vision

EYFS

Turns head in response to sounds and sights.

Adults can... Help babies to become aware of their own bodies through touch and movement, e.g. clapping the baby's hands together, gently shaking baby's foot.

Head towards light

Level 2: He will turn his head towards a light and will gaze at the human face, beginning to seek eye contact when at about arm's length away.

Level 3: His eyes scan the near environment, appearing to try to fix his gaze, contrasting light and dark. He will follow a shiny object through a range of about a quarter of a circle.

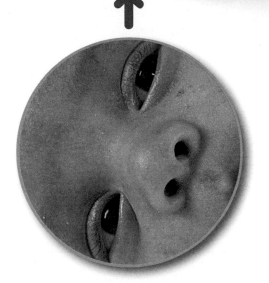

Eyes tracking toy

Level 2: He will track a toy with his eyes.

Level 3: He will become more and more aware of his body through interaction with his main carer.

Personal, social and emotional development

Key debate

Goldschmied and Jackson (1994, p. 37) believe that as babies and children do not yet have the language to tell us how they feel, they are very much in need of special relationships which are immediately 'there' for them in a concrete way.

What do you think is meant by the phrase 'in a concrete way'?

He/she:

➤ usually calms down when picked up
➤ may enjoy being cuddled
➤ enjoys sucking thumb/fingers/dummy
➤ is starting to show awareness of their surroundings.

Activity

Level 2 students will first be taught how to hold a baby and will be supervised at all times. Soon, practitioners become aware that babies often have a preferred way of being held. Try holding them over the shoulder or in a baby sling. Try playing quiet and soothing music when baby is awake and try dancing with them in your arms to the music. Swaying and gentle rocking movements are often preferred. Which movements do they seem to enjoy most?

EYFS

Enjoys the company of others and seeks contact with others from birth.

Adults can... Tune in sensitively to babies, and provide warm, loving, consistent care, responding quickly to babies' needs.

Gazing at carer

Level 2: She is beginning to seek eye contact at arm's length.

Level 3: Research shows that human faces are very attractive to babies.

Communication and language development

Key debate

Professor Colwyn Trevarthen showed how babies are ready and able to communicate. He studied babies and their mothers and observed the communication and movements between the babies and mothers.

He/she:

➤ is startled at loud sounds
➤ silences to soft rhythmic sounds
➤ turns their head towards carer's/an adult's voice
➤ has several cries for different reasons
➤ cries energetically for their needs to be met
➤ grunts and squeaks when content
➤ will take it in turns to vocalise with their carer
➤ may imitate a carer's expressions – such as poking out the tongue and smiling.

Activity

A good communication activity to try at this age is a simple one: when baby is alert, pick them up and start to talk to them about what's going on around them. At first this will feel strange and you might feel self-conscious but persist as this is a valuable beginning for baby. Or, try talking to baby in a different tone of voice. How do they react to a high-pitched voice? Then try using a lower tone of voice. Compare and record your findings.

Communicates needs and feelings in a variety of ways including crying, gurgling, babbling and squealing.

Adults can... Find out from parents how they like to communicate with their baby, noting especially the chosen language.

Baby crying

Level 2: She will try to make eye contact and cry in an attempt to communicate her needs.

Level 3: She cries in response to her developing sense of concepts such as hunger.

Intellectual and sensory development

He/she:

➤ shows recognition of familiar faces
➤ quietens when hearing familiar voices
➤ is startled by loud sounds
➤ gazes at patterns, particularly contrasts (black on white) and face patterns.

Activity

When baby is awake and alert, try making different shapes with your mouth and watch how they attempt to copy you. When baby is settled, you will notice how alert they are and how they appear keen to watch things that are nearby.

Choose a toy and try moving it slowly before them – watch their interest in it as it moves.

Reacts in interaction with others by smiling, looking and moving.

Adults can... Being physically close, making eye contact, using touch or voice all provide ideal opportunities for early conversations between adults and babies, and between one baby and another.

Face to face with carer

Level 2: She is likely to try to copy an adult opening her mouth wide.

Level 3: Baby seems to enjoy high-pitched, soothing sounds and will move her arms and legs.

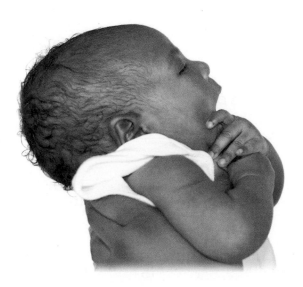

3 APPROACHING THREE MONTHS AND OVER

Video

Scan the QR code opposite to view a video demonstrating development for children approaching three months and over.
You can also access this video at http://tinyurl.com/aqjl3kg

Personal, social and emotional development

Key debate

'Attachment is a deep and enduring emotional bond that connects one person to another across time and space'

(Ainsworth, 1973; Bowlby, 1969)

Try researching more of Ainsworth's and Bowlby's theories and discuss the possible impact of the way in which a carer interacts positively with a baby of three months.

He/she:

➤ enjoys routines which are beginning to become familiar, such as bath time
➤ smiles
➤ still fixes their gaze on carers who feed them and are speaking around them.

Activity

Finger puppets are fascinating at this age. Try making the finger puppets sing and dance and watch his response. Record your findings.

EYFS

Seeks physical and emotional comfort by snuggling in to trusted adults.

Adults can… Use calming processes such as rocking or hugging.

Dad cuddling baby

Level 2: Baby shows enjoyment when cuddled or when receiving affection.

Level 3: Skin-to-skin contact releases a hormone called oxytocin, which promotes bonding.

Physical development

Key debate

Jean Piaget, a psychologist, described the period of time between birth and two years as the sensorimotor stage. He believed that the baby's behaviour was limited to simple motor responses caused by stimulation of the senses.

Do you think that is correct or are there other factors to take into account?

Inclusion point

A baby with visual impairment may benefit from a variety of toys and rattles which have smooth and solid surfaces (at this age, other textures can be baffling).

Gross motor skills

He/she:

➤ lies on their back, moving arms and legs alternately or together
➤ when held in a sitting position and supported, holds their head mostly without a droop and their back is beginning to straighten.

Neck and head control

Level 2: His neck and head control is developing.

Level 3: He can raise his head and chest and extend arms when lying on tummy (prone position).

Fine motor skills

He/she:

➤ brings their hands together
➤ can clasp and unclasp hands
➤ can move their head, following adult's/carer's movements.

Sitting with help

Level 2: He can sit with careful support.

Level 3: He can now hold his head without a droop. However, it occasionally bobs and his back is curved.

Holding rattle

Level 2: He will turn his head towards a sound such as a rattle.

Level 3: He responds by turning her head towards sounds that are beginning to be routine – such as bath time.

Activity

Offer baby a colourful rattle and watch how he attempts to moves his whole body and/or arm to get near it.

Inclusion point

Muscle tone may vary in a baby with, for example, spina bifida or cerebral palsy. Support baby in ways so that they too can enjoy a rattle and other stimulating toys.

EYFS

Makes movements with arms and legs which gradually become more controlled.

Adults can… Play games, such as offering a small toy and taking it again to rattle or sail through the air.

Communication and language development

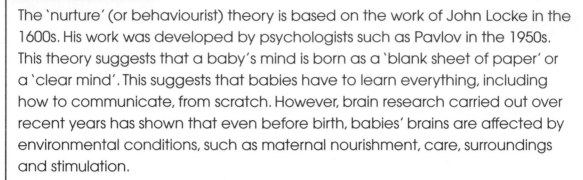

Key debate

The 'nurture' (or behaviourist) theory is based on the work of John Locke in the 1600s. His work was developed by psychologists such as Pavlov in the 1950s. This theory suggests that a baby's mind is born as a 'blank sheet of paper' or a 'clear mind'. This suggests that babies have to learn everything, including how to communicate, from scratch. However, brain research carried out over recent years has shown that even before birth, babies' brains are affected by environmental conditions, such as maternal nourishment, care, surroundings and stimulation.

Try researching other theorists who support this view.

He/she:

➤ is starting to coo and gurgle
➤ can vary their tone and volume
➤ smiles in response to attention
➤ cries noisily for needs to be met.

Activity

Babies tend to like nursery and action rhymes. 'Round and round the garden' has delighted babies for many years. See how a three-month-old baby responds to the fun.

Inclusion point

It is important for babies who are partially sighted to experience toys that are brightly coloured and interesting to touch. To support blind and partially sighted babies, also try toys that make a noise.

Makes own sounds in response when talked to by familiar adults.

Adults can… Ensure parents understand the importance of talking with babies in their home language.

Laughing

Level 2: He is starting to laugh.

Level 3: He can exchange chuckles with a familiar person and enjoys social interaction.

Intellectual and sensory development

Key debate

In 2011, researchers from the Institute of Psychiatry King's College London found that babies as young as three months are able to tune in to the sound of human voices and even recognise different emotions, even when they are asleep. Why do you think the human voice is so important to a young baby?

He/she:
➤ shows an increase of interest in playthings
➤ searches colourful mobiles and shiny objects with alert eyes
➤ is starting to understand cause and effect; for example, if they throw something down, it will make a sound.

Activity

When baby is in an alert state, change their position frequently so they have different things to watch and take an interest in. Colourful mobiles and soothing sing-song-type sounds are usually captivating for a baby of this age.

EYFS

Reacts in interaction with others by smiling, looking and moving.

Adults can… Display photographs showing how young babies communicate.

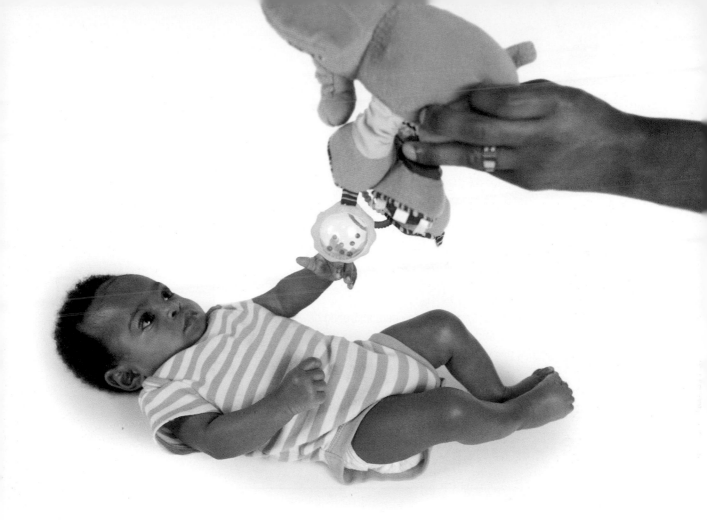

Eyes focusing on toy

Level 2: His eyes are beginning to focus together for some of the time.

Level 3: He uses a steady gaze towards an adult's eyes, in order to attract and hold their attention.

Video

Scan the QR code opposite to view a video demonstrating development for children approaching six months and over.

You can also access this video at http://tinyurl.com/bds34vp

Personal, social and emotional development

Key debate

Developmental psychologist Erick Erikson was interested in how children socialise and how this affects their sense of self. He developed a theory of psychosocial development in the 1950s.

In your opinion, how important is the development of trust based on the quality of the child's caregivers?

He/she:

➤ is mostly friendly to strangers but can be shy
➤ becomes upset when main carer leaves
➤ is starting to want to join in active games, such as pat-a-cake
➤ deliberately seeks attention
➤ is starting to cooperate with dressing, for example, by pushing arms into sleeves
➤ is more aware of others' feelings, e.g. people/children crying or laughing
➤ offers their toys to others
➤ can feed themselves with their fingers.

Activity

A mirror can offer no end of fascination to a baby of this age. Just at a time when they are developing a sense of 'who' they are, the chance to begin to recognise themselves in the mirror is a good way to begin. You might find baby tries to touch the reflection (obviously take care with mirrors for reasons of safety).

Inclusion point

Babies who seem unresponsive emotionally at this age may need extra support. Attempt to gain their attention by using songs and rhymes and try to engage them through eye contact.

Babies with a hearing impairment can benefit from toys that create vibrations that they can feel. Loud, rattling-type toys can be useful.

Looking at a book

Level 2: He can play alone for very short periods.

Level 3: He explores objects with both hands.

EYFS

Calms from being upset when held, rocked, spoken or sung to with soothing voice.

Adults can... Find out as much as you can from parents about young babies before they join the setting, so that the routines you follow are familiar and comforting.

Physical development

Gross motor skills

He/she:

- ➤ can roll from front to back and back to front
- ➤ can support themselves using their arms while lifting their head and chest when lying down
- ➤ holds up their arms to help with being picked up
- ➤ has a straighter back when held standing
- ➤ can take more of their weight on their legs if held in support
- ➤ shows a desire to be mobile
- ➤ kicks their legs with strength and alternates them.

Fine motor skills

He/she:

➤ grasps their foot when lying on their back
➤ will use an index finger to poke at small objects
➤ puts many objects in their mouth
➤ can pass a toy from one hand to the other hand
➤ can grab a toy within easy reach.

Activity

With new skills, such as reaching objects, try offering them brightly coloured bricks and stacking toys. Note how they respond when you smile and join in with the fun of their newly found abilities.

Fine motor skills

Level 2: He uses his whole hand to hold or take a toy/ object.

Level 3: This is called a palmar grasp.

Inclusion point

If baby is slower to reach and grab toys and rattles, persist by getting their attention by singing and then offering the toys to them.

Sitting unsupported

Level 2: He can sit unsupported for a few seconds and leans forward to maintain the position.

Level 3: He likes to adjust his position to see something of interest.

EYFS

Watches and explores hands and feet, e.g. when lying on back lifts legs into vertical position and grasps feet.

Adults can… Play games, such as offering a small toy and taking it again to rattle or sail through the air.

Playing with objects

Level 2: He can now reach for a toy as well as grabbing it.

Level 3: By now he may well transfer an object from one hand to another with ease.

Communication and language development

Key debate

According to psychologist Abraham Maslow, the human need for safety must be met before growth and development occur in other areas.

Discuss ways in which babies around this age can be helped to feel 'safe' and how it might contribute to their communication and language development.

He/she:

➤ uses a wide range of sounds
➤ laughs and screams
➤ can imitate some sounds
➤ uses a sing-song voice
➤ shakes toys to help them make a noise
➤ can understand 'up' and 'down'
➤ says 'ga, ga'
➤ will probably understand meaning of words 'mama' and 'dada'.

Activity

Offer noisy toys and watch baby make sense of the toys. Note which ones they enjoy and the sounds that attract them.

Turning to hear voice

Level 2: He turns to hear carer's voice – even when they are a little distance away.

Level 3: He indicates that he understands the meaning of the words by his actions, for example will wave bye-bye.

EYFS

Lifts arms in anticipation of being picked up.

Adults can… Encourage babies' sounds and babbling by copying their sounds in a turn-taking 'conversation'.

Intellectual and sensory development

Key debate

Baby sign language has recently been presented as a useful way of communicating with baby at this age. The usefulness appears to be due to hand–eye coordination developing sooner than verbal skills.

Inclusion point

Makaton and Signalong are commonly used. These are adapted from British Sign Language (BSL), but simplified to better suit the motor skills of very young children or those with motor control difficulties.

He/she:
➤ shows interest in picture books with bold pictures
➤ understands some words
➤ looks around a room with interest – eyes follow people's actions.

Activity

Try filling several containers with different objects, such as rice, stones etc. Then see how baby shakes each container and responds to the sounds they make.

Shaking a toy that makes a sound

Level 2: Repeats actions that have an effect, e.g. shaking a toy that makes a sound.

Level 3: This is an early step towards learning cause and effect.

EYFS

Quietens or alerts to the sound of speech.

Adults can… Encourage playfulness, turn-taking and responses, including peek-a-boo and rhymes.

5 APPROACHING NINE MONTHS AND OVER

Video

Scan the QR code opposite to view a video demonstrating development for children approaching nine months and over.

You can also access this video at http://tinyurl.com/a7a8f7q

Personal, social and emotional development

Key debate

Professor Colwyn Trevarthen discusses how singing to babies provides emotional stability. He also believes that music provides clues, together with a sense of what is going on, even when babies do not understand the words. He has studied how musical games, songs and stories support the development of early skills.

Choose a variety of genres of music and discover which ones baby appears to enjoy most.

He/she:

➤ shows greater interest in social interaction
➤ enjoys songs and rhymes
➤ is becoming cautious of strangers
➤ is beginning to assert themselves, e.g. shows annoyance by stiffening their body
➤ may be attached to a comforter
➤ enjoys social time during meals.

Comfort object

Level 2: She enjoys the comfort of her favourite toys.

Level 3: Some textures are comforting to the young child.

Activity

Bath time can be great fun at this age. Try offering them sponges, funnels, squeaky ducks and beakers.

EYFS

Shows a range of emotions such as pleasure, fear and excitement.

Adults can... Be close by and available, to ensure that babies feel safe and loved even when they are not the centre of adult attention.

Physical development

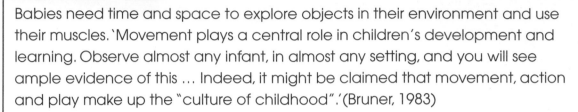

Gross motor skills

He/she:

➤ may pull themselves up to standing using furniture, but cannot lower themselves afterwards
➤ reaches out for toys
➤ flaps arms up and down when excited
➤ can sit securely without support and with a straight back for short periods of time.

Crawling attempt

Level 2: She will find different ways to move, e.g. crawl, wriggle along on tummy or roll.

Level 3: Greater mobility offers her the freedom to explore and experience more.

Fine motor skills

He/she:

➤ can hold finger food
➤ manipulates toys with interest.

Grasping objects

Level 2: She can grasp objects between finger and thumb (pincer grasp).

Level 3: She can release a toy from her own grasp but only by dropping it or passing it to another hand.

Activity

Music is stimulating for baby and they will love to bounce and sway while laughing. Try different types of music. Which do they like best?

EYFS

Reaches out for, touches and begins to hold objects.

Adults can... Encourage young babies in their efforts to gradually share control of the bottle with you (although many babies will be drinking from a two-handled beaker rather than a bottle at this stage).

Communication and language development

Key debate

Noam Chomsky (the linguist philosopher) proposed that all humans have a language acquisition device (LAD), which means that children are born with the capacity for language development. However, researchers now consider how language also develops in response to the environment. For example, in some sad cases of severe neglect this has resulted in gaps in a child's language ability.

How would you describe a rich language environment for a child?

Looking at a book

Level 2: She enjoys colourful books with bold pictures and can recognise familiar pictures in books.

Level 3: Understanding pictures is one of the first steps towards understanding symbols and words.

He/she:

➤ listens carefully to the voices of familiar carers
➤ shouts
➤ makes the sounds: 'mm' 'gg' 'dd' 'brr'
➤ responds to the word 'no' by stopping
➤ can copy an adult cough
➤ will understand very simple instructions such as 'hug mummy'.

Activity

Share a variety of books with baby. Try ones that pop up or have flaps as these are fascinating to them. Share in the joy of wondering what might happen next and laugh with them as they show surprise.

EYFS

Practises and gradually develops speech sounds (babbling) to communicate with adults; says sounds like 'baba', 'nono', 'gogo'.

Adults can... Communicate with parents to exchange and update information about babies' personal words.

Intellectual and sensory development

He/she:

➤ shows understanding and recognition of daily routines.

Activity

Sensory activities are exciting for babies around this age. Try to provide materials of different textures for them to touch and feel. Of course, they will want to put them in their mouths, so every item needs to be washed or cleaned. Fruits and vegetables that are not 'squashy' are the best and can be a good place to start. Remember to maintain health and safety standards throughout and observe the babies' actions/reactions.

How do you think that this activity might also contribute to their acceptance of a variety of foods in the future?

Hidden toy

Level 2: She understands more about object permanence: watches a toy being hidden and then she will look for it.

Level 3: At four to eight months, she will reach for an object that is partially hidden. Then around eight months, she watches a toy being hidden in one place and will look for it.

EYFS

Moves whole body to sounds they enjoy, such as music or a regular beat.

Adults can... Use a lively voice, with ups and downs to help babies tune in.

6 APPROACHING ONE YEAR AND OVER

Video

Scan the QR code opposite to view a video demonstrating development for children approaching one year and over.

You can also access this video at http://tinyurl.com/ab9zdsq

Personal, social and emotional development

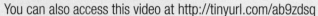

Key debate

Malaguzzi (1993) believes that creativity becomes more obvious and visible when adults value the process rather than just the end result.

How important do you think materials are which don't have a specific outcome, such as empty cardboard boxes?

He/she:

➤ can be assertive
➤ likes a comfort cloth, blanket or thumb
➤ likes to see brothers and sisters and other familiar people approaching
➤ can help with daily routines, e.g. puts their foot out for sock
➤ enjoys trying to feed themselves.

Being shy

Level 2: She may show shyness towards strangers.

Level 3: She likes to have a carer close by for security.

Activity

Now is the time to help them get creative. Try offering them large pieces of paper and thick crayons and consider using natural materials such as sand and water. Messy play and imaginative play materials indoors and outdoors will provide the variety of materials they need at this stage.

Inclusion point

Children need to feel included in creative activities, regardless of their ability. As there is no right or wrong way to use water, sand, dough, paint or crayons (the outcome is not fixed) then children can explore and succeed at their own pace.

Comfort toy

Level 2: His favourite toy also offers comfort.

Level 3: 'Transitional objects' such as a blanket or soft toy can provide a sense of security.

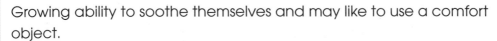

EYFS

Growing ability to soothe themselves and may like to use a comfort object.

Adults can... Make sure the key person (the key worker system gives babies and toddlers individual attention to their needs at times they can expect) stays close by and provides a secure presence and a refuge at times when a child may be feeling anxious.

Coping with emotions

Level 2: Her moods are inconsistent as she hasn't learned how to manage her emotions yet.

Level 3: She is emotionally labile (this means that she will probably have alternating moods).

Physical development

Gross motor skills

He/she:

➤ can sit securely for a long period
➤ can get up to sit from lying down position
➤ can sit from standing position
➤ can get up to stand without any support
➤ may be able to stand for a few seconds
➤ will go from crawling to bottom shuffling or cruising along furniture and back to walking
➤ can crawl upstairs
➤ may throw toys using whole arm.

Walking alone

Level 2: He may be able to walk without holding on.

Level 3: Feet are usually wide apart and hands are usually raised to help balance.

Fine motor skills

He/she:

➤ can hold their cup or bottle
➤ is able to release a toy deliberately from their hand

- tries to shuffle food onto a spoon
- can steer spoon to their mouth but often misses
- uses a fine pincer grasp (grasping an object between the thumb and forefinger) to pick up small objects
- turns several pages in one go
- may begin to show a preference for using one hand in particular.

Activity

Bath-time play has so many benefits for this age group. It can serve as a time to experiment with water and chat together, and also provides a way for them to wind down. Try alternating the toys each week so they have something different to play with.

Inclusion point

If baby is unable to sit and there is an identified developmental delay, still encourage them to take part in bath-time play and take it very much at their pace. It is important to remember to adapt any activity to meet the child's individual needs.

EYFS

Takes first few steps independently.

Adults can... Be aware that babies have little sense of danger when their interests are focused on getting something they want.

Grasping pen

Level 2: She holds an item such as a pen in a palmer grasp.

Level 3: She will enjoy using a range of mark-making materials to ignite further creativity.

Communication and language development

He/she:

➤ babbles tunefully
➤ may speak two or more recognisable words
➤ may use the word for an object or part of the word when trying to communicate about something they want
➤ understands everyday words, for example, bath, bottle, dog
➤ tries to join in with conversations.

Handing teddy to adult

Level 2: She understands instructions such as 'Hand teddy to me'.

Level 3: She is beginning to understand the use of objects and handle them in an appropriate way, e.g. knows that a bowl is to eat out of and a teddy is to hug.

Pointing and looking

Level 2: She draws attention to things of interest to her by pointing.

Level 3: A carer's response to her interest stimulates language development.

Activity

There are several inexpensive activities that can encourage language development within this age group. Share picture books with them; find cuddly toys which you can pretend to make talk to them. Or find a range of music to dance and clap to; build up several treasure baskets which contain lots of natural materials (constant supervision needed); play peek-a-boo with them; sing rhymes to them.

Inclusion point

Watch their reactions to sounds and be aware of any potential hearing loss.

EYFS

Frequently imitates words and sounds.

Adults can... When babies try to say a word, repeat it back so they can hear the name of the object clearly.

Intellectual and sensory development

Key debate

Similarly to Piaget, Bruner believed that right from birth children can begin to make sense of the world. However, unlike Piaget, Bruner argued that the child's social world influences intellectual development.

What sort of social activity do you think a baby of around one year of age might enjoy?

He/she:

➤ draws attention to things that interest them – objects and toys particularly
➤ begins to enjoy role play, perhaps feeding teddy with their spoon
➤ understands what familiar everyday objects can do
➤ understands simple commands such as 'give me the ball'
➤ shows persistence – tries and tries again when they can't do things
➤ learns through trial and error.

Activity

Try playing together making pretend calls on toy telephones; listen to how they copy the tone of your voice.

EYFS

Concentrates intently on an object or activity of own choosing for short periods.

Adults can… Share favourite stories as babies are settling to sleep, or at other quiet times.

Pointing to part of body

Level 2: He can point to parts of his body when asked (e.g. 'Where is your head?).

Level 3: Comprehension precedes articulation.

7 APPROACHING 18 MONTHS AND OVER

Video

Scan the QR code opposite to view a video demonstrating development for children approaching 18 months and over.
You can also access this video at http://tinyurl.com/b7pgbkp

Personal, social, emotional development

Key debate

Recently, theorists, such as Bob Hughes (2011), Gordon Sturrock and Perry Else (1998) have been looking more closely at play where it is helped along by adults but without unnecessary involvement in the play itself. How important do you think is to provide bright and colourful play equipment?

He/she:

➤ is developing a stronger sense of who she is
➤ often cries 'me do it', showing that she is keen to develop a little independence.

Activity

Heuristic play (collections of natural materials, such as conkers, fir cones and seashells, alongside ribbons, jar lids and cardboard tubes) is fascinating – children get to explore materials that have different textures (too much plastic can seem boring!). Of course, safety is an issue with small items but with an adult sitting close by keeping a watchful eye, the experiments can begin…).

Inclusion point

Children with a range of special needs particularly enjoy stimulating materials (a multi-sensory room is ideal) but in a small way a basket filled to the brim with interesting objects can work well too.

18-month-old engaged in solo (or solitary) play

Level 2: She plays by herself with an adult close by.

Level 3: She enjoys solo play and is within Piaget's egocentric stage of development.

18-month-old having tantrum

Level 2: She is coming to terms with frustrating things in her life, which often gives way to tantrums.

Level 3: As time passes, she will learn how to express herself appropriately and tantrums will lessen.

EYFS

Is aware of others' feelings, for example looks concerned if hears crying or looks excited if hears a familiar happy voice.

Adults can... Help young children to label emotions such as sadness or happiness, by talking to them about their own feelings and those of others.

Mimicking animal sounds

Level 2: She will probably love playing with puppets.

Level 3: She can follow rhymes that include repetition – using puppets to tell the stories will help hold her concentration.

Physical development

Key debate

Harry and Margaret Harlow working in the 1960s and 1970s carried out experiments on young monkeys. They found that the monkeys who did not receive physical contact suffered emotionally and socially. They also found that when they released the monkeys back into the company of monkeys brought up normally, they couldn't join in the everyday rough-and-tumble games.

Inclusion point

Why do you think emotional comfort and physical contact for children in the early years might be so important?

Walking steadily

Level 2: She is starting to walk steadily.

Level 3: Greater level of balance and coordination allows her to walk more confidently and she may like to carry or drag things behind her.

Gross motor skills

He/she:

➤ walks confidently, can stop when they want without stumbling
➤ enjoys walking and carrying their toys
➤ bends down without falling over
➤ enjoys pulling and pushing large toys
➤ can climb forwards into a chair and then turn around to sit.

Fine motor skills

He/she:

➤ can hold a pencil in their palm, or they may start to use their thumb and first two fingers in a primitive tripod grasp
➤ enjoys making dots and can move the pencil up and down and side to side
➤ uses paintbrush, using their arm to make long strokes.

Activity

At 18 months, they are curious about everything and want to 'have a go', so letting them explore their developing physical skills in a safe way is important. Try rotating a range of daily activities, which will build their strength in different areas. On one day you could provide materials that encourage them to push and pull and on another focus on activities that encourage 'posting' items (e.g. long cardboard tubes and small objects to post).

Spoon to mouth

Level 2: She can use a spoon to feed herself.

Level 3: She can hold a spoon between her thumb and first two fingers. This is called the primitive tripod grasp.

EYFS

Makes connections between their movement and the marks they make.

Adults can... Encourage independence as young children explore particular patterns of movement, sometimes referred to as schemas.

Creative play

Level 2: She can remove small objects from larger objects such as containers or bottles by turning them upside down.

Level 3: She can now control the movement of her wrists, which she can use to shape objects such as dough.

Communication and language development

He/she:

➤ chatters and jabbers
➤ may echo the last spoken words of an adult (echolalia)
➤ may put two words together (telegraphese). For example, 'Cat come', 'More juice'
➤ can respond to simple commands such as 'Give the teddy to me'
➤ uses words together with gestures
➤ likes to say 'no!'
➤ refers to themselves by name
➤ uses around 30 words, (some whole words and some partial) but understands much more
➤ can join in with nursery rhymes and songs.

Activity

Pictures of items from the real word (preferably photographs), whether they are shown on a poster, in a book, on an iPad or computer, are fascinating for babies. They offer a range of things for a carer to talk about. You will find that the 18-month-old will want to point at ones they are interested in.

EYFS

Copies familiar expressions, e.g. 'Oh dear', 'All gone'.

Adults can... Build vocabulary by giving choices and asking, e.g. 'apple or satsuma?' Ask open-ended questions too.

Dancing

Level 2: She will try to join in with rhymes.

Level 3: Music and movement are an important form of communication.

Intellectual development

He/she:

➤ is really curious and determined to understand as much as possible
➤ happily sits looking at picture books, trying to name objects
➤ places objects in and out of containers
➤ concentrates on one activity at a time – ignoring everything else.

Playing with puppet

Level 2: She learns about the world through suitable play activities.

Level 3: 'Play is a child's work.' (Piaget) She will concentrate for long periods on activities that fascinate her.

Activity

Try telling them a story while using a puppet. Then offer them the puppet and observe the way they play.

EYFS

Has a strong exploratory impulse.

Adults can... Create an environment which invites responses from babies and adults, for example touching, smiling, smelling, feeling, listening, exploring, describing and sharing.

8 APPROACHING TWO YEARS AND OVER

Video

Scan the QR code opposite to view a video demonstrating development for children approaching two years and over.
You can also access this video at http://tinyurl.com/bx4v5bl

Personal, emotional and social development

Key debate

Erikson's theory of psychological development identifies a period between one and three years where children begin to want their independence. The point is made that with encouragement children become more secure in their ability to survive in the world.

How do you think adults can balance the need to keep children safe while allowing them greater freedom?

Inclusion point

Also, how important might it be for a practitioner to recognise a need for greater independence and make ways for this to be possible for all children, regardless of their disability or special educational needs?

Special note: When a child is aged between two and three, practitioners must review their progress and provide parents and/or carers with a short written summary of their child's development in the prime areas. Each child's level of development must be addressed against their progress towards the Early Learning Goals for the three prime areas. Students and practitioners should also refer to the EYFS Development Matters materials for guidance.

He/she:

➤ likes to parallel play (play alongside others) and may start to join in
➤ enjoys playing with objects and pretending they are something else, for example a box
➤ begins to share experiences with others, but sharing toys can present a problem
➤ is friendly and affectionate to others
➤ may build a special friendship with another child
➤ wants to try out new things and do things immediately
➤ is learning to separate from main carer for short periods
➤ can part dress themselves on their own
➤ sways from being independent to being clingy
➤ expresses own likes and dislikes
➤ may often have tantrums.

Activity

Two-year-olds love to see photos of when they were younger and may enjoy looking at photos of family members. Try making books of people and places that are familiar to the child, e.g. park, nursery, house etc., and chat with them about how they feel they have grown and the things they can do now. This is a good activity for boosting confidence.

Looking at photographs

Level 2: He can appreciate how he has developed and grown.

Level 3: He begins to show empathy towards others and understands that some actions may upset others.

Inclusion point

For a child with hearing impairment at this age, be sure to make eye contact first and then use gestures to reinforce your communication about how they have developed (perhaps to demonstrate how they have grown in height). Don't be tempted to raise your voice – gestures work well.

EYFS

Tries to help or give comfort when others are distressed.

Adults can... Help children to recognise when their actions hurt others.

Play time

Level 2: He may often play on his own – this is called solitary play.

Level 3: He may often like to watch other children play – this is called 'spectator play'.

Physical development

Children around this age enjoy attempting to kick a large ball. They will also run safely now and may climb fairly confidently.

Key debate

Vygotsky's zone of proximal development is all about getting it right for the child in terms of what a child can do and what the next step could be.

Discuss what sort of physical activity a child could be offered to help 'bridge' that 'gap'.

Inclusion point

All children need time to rehearse and practise new skills. It is important to allow plenty of time when a child has low self-esteem or learning difficulties.

Gross motor skills

He/she:

➤ runs safely
➤ squats with steadiness and rises to feet without using hands
➤ may be able to stand on tiptoe
➤ jumps with both feet together
➤ uses stairs – both feet to each step
➤ climbs confidently
➤ tries to kick a large ball but usually walks into it
➤ can throw a ball but can't catch
➤ uses tricycle and may be able to use peddles
➤ pushes and pulls things on wheels.

Fine motor skills

He/she:

➤ turns pages in books
➤ picks up small objects, using fine pincer grasp
➤ builds a tower of seven or more blocks
➤ uses mark-making tools such as chubby crayons
➤ can make circular shapes and lines with fingers in paints, sand, shaving foam etc.

Inclusion point

If a child has coordination difficulties, see if they are able to continue. If not, a little support often goes a long way to helping them enjoy their achievements. Also, make a note to observe the child again when undertaking a similar activity and begin to build up an overall picture of the child's development. Share the information with your supervisor or manager.

EYFS

Climbs confidently and is beginning to pull themselves up on nursery climbing equipment.

Adults can... Be aware that children can be very energetic for short bursts and need periods of rest and relaxation.

Hoola Hoop play

Level 2: Two-year-olds enjoy being active and are full of energy.

Level 3: At this age, curiosity drives them to explore the world and they love to find out what their bodies can achieve!

Communication and language development

He/she:

➤ enjoys using sounds, songs and rhymes in play

➤ names people and objects

➤ understands and copies simple sentences

➤ is beginning to ask simple questions

➤ is learning words rapidly and can use up to 200 words

➤ understands a vast amount of words, around 1,000 (more than they can pronounce)

➤ may begin to use 'I', 'me' and 'you' correctly

➤ is likely to ask 'what?', 'when?' and 'who?'

➤ can use action words such as 'go' and 'out'

➤ is likely to mistakenly place similar things into the same category, e.g. pointing to any four-legged animal and saying that it is a dog

➤ may still like to repeat over and over what they have heard someone say (echololia).

Using gesture to communicate

Level 2: She may talk to herself while playing, apparently telling herself what to do!

Level 3: She uses fingers for songs and rhymes (e.g. Incy Wincy Spider).

Activity

Try providing children with a range of recyclable materials that make a variety of sounds. Note how the children use the sounds to communicate their thoughts and feelings.

Inclusion point

A child with visual impairment may particularly enjoy recycled materials that have a variety of textures. Start to collect a variety of materials they could experience in future activities.

EYFS

Learns new words very rapidly and is able to use them in communicating.

Adults can... Follow the child's lead to talk about what they are interested in.

Intellectual development

Key debate

Tina Bruce (1997) discussed schemas as being a cluster of pieces that fit together. 'Schemas are patterns of linked behaviours, which the child can generalise and use in a whole variety of different situations.'

Inclusion point

Children with special educational needs and disabilities may need support in expressing their preferred schema at any moment in time. Watch out for opportunities to provide great equipment for them.

He/she:

➤ begins to understand consequence of actions, for example an object falling over may break
➤ begins to understand and respond to humour
➤ follows simple instructions/requests
➤ knows their full name
➤ points out more and more detail in a book and will search for favourite characters
➤ likes to look at photographs of family and friends and is beginning to recognise themselves in photos
➤ is gaining confidence to try new activities with adult support
➤ can talk about an object that should be there, e.g. 'The toy box usually has my teddy in it.'

Two-year-old trying out enveloping schema

Level 2: She enjoys exploring schemas.

Level 3: A child may choose an enveloping schema. Others may enjoy different ones.

Activity

Try supporting a child's preferred schema. For example, offer them recycled materials such as wrapping paper to wrap things up if they are interested in an enveloping schema (which is all about a fascination with putting things into things, such as bags or filling wheelbarrows). If the child has a trajectory schema (fascination with things that go up and down) then try providing different safe items for them to throw (e.g. bean bags and soft balls).

EYFS

Beginning to organise and categorise objects, e.g. putting all the teddy bears together or teddies and cars in separate piles.

Adults can... Talk to young children about 'lots' and 'few' as they play.

9 APPROACHING THREE YEARS AND OVER

Video

Scan the QR code opposite to view a video demonstrating development for children approaching three years and over.
You can also access this video at http://tinyurl.com/a8a2n4q

Personal, social and emotional development

At this age, children are generally more helpful to adults. They are getting better at doing things more independently too.

Key debate

Bruner (1966) believed that as children develop they use different ways of representing the world around them.

Inclusion point

Children with autism also need to engage in activities that allow them to represent the world. How could a practitioner begin to help them?

He/she:

- is better at expressing their feelings with words
- begins cooperative play (starts to understand rules, willing to share and take turns)
- shows more affection to younger children
- plays in a more imaginative way, which can, in turn, lead to the development of fears
- is aware of gender roles
- is learning to cope better with their emotions
- believes that all rules are fixed.

Helping to put toys away

Level 2: She enjoys helping adults.

Level 3: She likes doing things all by herself and this need for independence is crucial to ongoing confidence.

Activity

Find a variety of pictures or photos of children showing basic emotions, such as happy, sad and angry, and talk to the child about them.

Inclusion point

Malleable materials such as dough and gloop (cornflower and water) are great ways for children with behavioural challenges to release their feelings in a safe way.

EYFS

Can usually adapt behaviour to different events, social situations and changes in routine.

Adults can... Collaborate with children in creating explicit rules for the care of the environment.

Talking about emotions

Level 2: He enjoys routine, such as a set time of day for mealtimes.

Level 3: He has a better understanding of empathy, and can start to see situations from someone else's perspective.

Physical development

Key debate

Theorists such as Piaget, Dewey, Vygotsky, Donaldson and Bronfenbrenner (and recent research on brain development) support the theory that first-hand experiences help children's early learning and development. How do you see the adult role in supporting first-hand experiences?

Inclusion point

Early intervention when a developmental delay has been identified is an important aspect of the study of child development.

In your view, how should developmental delay be identified? Why should this process include a broader focus than just average age of achievement?

Gross motor skills

He/she:

➤ jumps from a low height
➤ walks in different directions, backwards and sideways
➤ can balance on one foot
➤ throws and catches a ball
➤ may be able to use pedals on tricycles
➤ has better spatial awareness (when moving around objects)
➤ can kick a ball.

Fine motor skills

He/she:

➤ can build towers of nine or ten bricks

➤ can make up and down and circular movements using tools such as pencils, paintbrushes, sticks in mud etc., which will lead into letter shapes, or can copy some letter shapes using tools and multi-sensory materials, e.g. paintbrushes in paint, sticks in sand

➤ is beginning to learn how to use safe scissors

➤ can paint with large brushes

➤ can use a fork and spoon to eat.

Activity

Set up a mini obstacle course using boxes and cushions and encourage children to 'have a go'.

Inclusion point

All children, regardless of ability, need to be challenged to reach their next step. You may like to keep a diary showing a child's personal journey so that you can plan their next step. Keep a note of progress and share with them their achievements.

On tiptoes

Level 2: She can stand and walk on tiptoes.

Level 3: She has an improved sense of coordination and balance.

Drawing

Level 2: He can draw a person: first come legs, then arms coming out of head.

Level 3: He is beginning to hold a pencil effectively in order to make marks and shapes. May not yet have a dynamic tripod grasp.

EYFS

Runs skilfully and negotiates space successfully, adjusting speed or direction to avoid obstacles.

Adults can... Talk about why children should take care when moving freely.

Jumping and climbing

Level 2: She can jump off a low step.

Level 3: She can climb stairs.

Communication and language development

Key debate

The Effective Provision of Pre-School Education (EPPE) Project (2003–2008) found that high quality pre-schooling is related to better intellectual and social/behavioural development for children.

What does the phrase 'quality of pre-school provision' mean to you and how can it be achieved?

Inclusion point

Children with hearing impairment can be provided with check points/visual clues around the nursery to improve their ability to be independent. For example, pictures of photos indicating the use of equipment can be helpful.

He/she:

➤ can hold simple conversations, missing odd words
➤ seeks to understand, often asking 'why?'
➤ is developing good listening skills, provided they are listened to patiently
➤ may stutter when very excited or nervous
➤ knows and can say up to several hundred words
➤ can link three or four words together in a sentence, but may miss out words such as 'and', 'the' and 'is'
➤ may ask for help
➤ may stop and start in sentences, trying to find the right word
➤ is starting to use verbs, such as 'run', eat'
➤ is starting to use adjectives such as 'small', 'clean'
➤ may start to learn more than one language, given the opportunity
➤ understands the difference between singular and plural.

Playing with musical instrument

Level 2: He begins to clap along to the beat and will enjoy moving with the rhythm.

Level 3: Music, songs, rhymes and instruments can become an essential tool for communicating how he feels.

Activity

Puppet play is a particularly effective way of connecting with young children.

Inclusion point

You may find that a child who is finding it hard to express themself in words will happily chat to a puppet. Puppets don't have to be expensive – making one out of an old sock can work just as well.

EYFS

Builds up vocabulary that reflects the breadth of their experiences.

Adults can... Introduce new words in the context of play and activities.

Intellectual development

He/she:

➤ enjoys learning new skills such as games on a computer
➤ can control their own attention when playing, stopping and starting at will
➤ is beginning to get a sense of time passing – the difference between present and past
➤ is starting to understand seasonal/weather changes
➤ often confuses fact and fiction and might insert an 'event' from a story into an event in their own life when recalling a situation
➤ is beginning to understand cause and effect and will ask 'why?'
➤ can match three primary colours.

Touching and counting shells

Level 2: He is starting to count one to ten but has yet to truly understand that one number equals one object. Says 'one' or 'lots'.

Level 3: He can sort objects into simple categories.

Activity

Encourage children to touch objects while saying the number and name by offering a variety of natural objects, such as shells or leaves. When a child touches an object and says the name and number, this is called 'tagging'. Also, try filling a sack with their favourite book together with simple objects from the book itself. For example, for Goldilocks and the three bears, pop in the book, three teddies, bowls and spoons and they are ready to play!

EYFS

Listens to stories with increasing attention and recall.

Adults can… Cue children, particularly those with communication difficulties, into a change of conversation, e.g. 'Now we are going to talk about…'.

10 APPROACHING FOUR YEARS AND OVER

Video

Scan the QR code opposite to view a video demonstrating development for children approaching four years and over.
You can also access this video at http://tinyurl.com/b9vb2jw

Personal, social and emotional development

At this age, children enjoy imaginative play and show a sense of humour. They can be strong willed and competitive too.

Key debate

Think about this developmental theory: Erikson identified a period during which children assert themselves more and with that new confidence comes a sense of being able to take the initiative. If this is not allowed to develop, children may develop a lack in self-initiative and a sense of guilt (feeling a burden to others).

Inclusion point

If a child has an identified condition, disability or impairment, how can a practitioner ensure this new area of development is allowed to take shape? What skills can the practitioner help to develop in the child to allow this to happen?

He/she:

➤ shows greater sensitivity and compassion towards others
➤ is strongly self-willed
➤ is beginning to understands how to cooperate with others
➤ enjoys demonstrating skills
➤ shows sense of humour
➤ likes the company of other children (associative play stage)
➤ still continues in solo play
➤ is trying to understand right and wrong
➤ is often involved in elaborate imaginative play.

Playing with water – washing hands

Level 2: He desires to be independent and can take part in simple self-care routines.

Level 3: Playing with therapeutic materials such as water helps to release emotions.

Activity

Provide children with a range of malleable materials, such as dough, sand or clay and note how it impacts their emotions. Record how their emotions or reactions change.

Inclusion point

A child with a learning disability should never be excluded from an activity; just remember that they may need a shorter session, or extra time to repeat new skills. Adapt the activity to meet the child's individual needs.

EYFS

Understands that their own actions affect other people, e.g. they become upset or try to comfort another child when they realise they have upset them.

Adults can... Talk about fair and unfair situations, children's feelings about fairness and how we can make things fair.

Sharing toys

Level 2: He is beginning to understand the importance of sharing.

Level 3: His moods are more stable but may still fluctuate.

Physical development

Gross motor skills

He/she:

➤ can stand or run on tiptoe
➤ can ride a tricycle, turning corners
➤ climbs over large apparatus, climbing frames etc.
➤ climbs stairs with confidence
➤ can run well: starting, stopping and turning corners with control
➤ has a good sense of balance, may be able to walk/run in straight lines
➤ can kick, throw, catch and bounce a ball
➤ bends instead of squats to pick up objects.

Drawing around fingers

Level 2: He can hold a pencil – just like an adult.

Level 3: He is showing increased fine motor skills and development of hand–eye coordination.

Fine motor skills

He/she:

➤ is starting to be able to form some letters, e.g. their name
➤ draws pictures that are more recognisable, e.g. fingers on hands.

Activity

Small fingers like to get moving when they are given the chance to explore new materials. Try offering a colourful sack or bag full of interesting recyclable odds and ends. Then encourage them to empty out the contents and think about what they could make. They might also enjoy feeling the different textures and talking about the materials.

Inclusion point

Children with coordination challenges should be given equal opportunities to develop their skills. Sometimes it can just be about lending a hand to steady the material or ensuring the child has sensory feedback during the activity – the success can be just as rewarding for the child.

EYFS

Usually dry and clean during the day.

Adults can... Acknowledge and encourage children's efforts to manage their personal needs and to use and return resources appropriately.

Jumping on a trampoline

Level 2: He is able to play and move around with less chance of falling over/ bumping into objects.

Level 3: He has improved spatial awareness.

Communication and language development

He/she:

➤ asks more questions: Why? When? How? Can I have? Can I go?
➤ can talk about future activities and what they will do
➤ loves jokes and absurdities, and sentences like 'A cow goes quack' will make them laugh
➤ might enjoy making words up
➤ tries to make grammatically irregular words fit grammatical rules, for example 'I goed' instead of 'I went'
➤ uses words such as 'in', 'on' and 'under'
➤ might find it difficult to pronounce sounds such as 'r', 'th' and 'str ' (in straw) or 'scr' (in scrap) and 'sp' (in crisps).

Activity

He/she can be helped to use an inexpensive digital camera (if possible) and it can be a great way for adults to see things from their perspective. Why not help a child photograph all the things that they like?

Inclusion point

Children with a range of communication difficulties may well find visual prompts a valuable way to express themselves.

Looking at a book

Level 2: He shows greater interest in text when reading books.

Level 3: He is likely to start recognising patterns in word formations, e.g. the past tense of 'walk' is 'walked' and the past tense of 'talk' is 'talked'. However, he won't be consistently able to apply these correctly, so will often get words and tenses wrong.

EYFS

Extends vocabulary, especially by grouping and naming, exploring the meanings and sounds of new words.

Adults can... Support children's growing ability to express a wide range of feelings orally and talk about their own experiences.

Intellectual development

Key debate

Friedrich Froebel, experimenting in the early years of the 19th century, concluded that a child's best thinking is done when they are playing. In your opinion, which play experiences that encourage children around this age to be physically active could have the kind of impact that Froebel was discussing?

Inclusion point

Keeping in mind that children should be physically active while learning, how can you make provision for physical interaction with the environment for a child who uses a wheelchair?

He/she:

➤ can say numbers up to ten and beyond (actual understanding of number may only be up to three) although many four-year-olds can accurately count and understand objects to ten)

➤ has a greater understanding of humour

➤ can match primary colours

➤ can solve some simple problems, such as where to look for a lost toy

➤ can give some simple reasons, such as the plate is empty because they ate all their food

➤ repeats songs/nursery rhymes

➤ has a greater focus of attention.

Activity

Role-play areas need to be offered indoors and outdoors. Try making a special waterproof storage box especially for outdoors. Place belts and hats in it and watch how the children use them. Children really enjoy experimenting with objects from everyday life as they can relate them to 'real' situations within their own lives.

Role play with dressing-up clothes

Level 2: He tells stories, listens to stories and enjoys role play.

Level 3: He may still confuse fact and fiction.

Inclusion point

If a child has an identified condition, disability or impairment, then to meet the inclusion requirements you must adapt an activity to ensure that all children can join in. Here's just one example: if the children are playing with sand, perhaps provide a smaller sand tray that they could use on their own, with adult support if required.

EYFS

Maintains attention, concentrates and sits quietly during appropriate activity.

Adults can... Explain why it is important to pay attention when others are speaking.

APPROACHING FIVE YEARS AND OVER

Video

Scan the QR code opposite to view a video demonstrating development for children approaching five years and over.
You can also access this video at http://tinyurl.com/a8wkoj2

Personal, social and emotional development

Key debate

Psychologist Albert Bandura (1977) proposed a theory of child development where children learn new behaviours from observing other people. Unlike behavioural theorists, Bandura believed that a sense of pride, satisfaction and accomplishment could also lead to learning.

How important do you think it is to offer praise and encouragement to children? Bear in mind that praise results in positive feelings and makes the original behaviour more likely to occur in the future.

Inclusion point

Children with learning or behavioural difficulties can be helped to cope with changes in routine or a change in focus of an activity if they are warned in advance. Signalling that an activity is about to change by using visual prompts (signs) and verbal prompts, e.g. 'now' and 'next' can be helpful.

He/she:

➤ displays kindness and sympathy
➤ builds one-to-one relationships
➤ plays cooperatively while solo play also continues
➤ shows interest in small-world play
➤ has definite likes and dislikes
➤ may continue to develop fears – either irrational or rational
➤ is developing self-awareness
➤ has a greater awareness of the opinions of others.

Using knife and fork

Level 2: He can understand routine.

Level 3: He is beginning to understand many social behaviours, for example mealtime conventions and how to greet someone.

Activity

Children need an environment that promotes cultural diversity. You may like to plan a display and interest table around a major festival. For example, there is a range of materials that can be gathered to represent Hanukkah, Chinese New Year, Easter or Diwali. The objects and pictures chosen can offer a springboard for discussion for children.

Caring for pet

Level 2: He is caring towards younger children and animals.

Level 3: He can entertain himself for longer periods of time.

EYFS

Aware of the boundaries set and of behavioural expectations in the setting.

Adults can... Ensure that children have opportunities to identify and discuss boundaries, so that they understand why the boundaries are there and what they are intended to achieve.

Empathy

Level 2: She is beginning to understand the needs of others, including animals.

Level 3: She will instinctively try to look after animals or children that are younger than her or who are distressed.

Physical development

Gross motor skills

He/she:

➤ enjoys throwing a ball but may still use their whole arm to catch it
➤ dances with rhythm to music
➤ climbs and swings on climbing frames, showing good balance and coordination
➤ can use a two-wheeled bike but usually needs stabilisers
➤ dresses without much supervision
➤ probably finds tying shoelaces a challenge.

Fine motor skills

He/she:

➤ can form many letters and numbers

- can use pencils, crayons and large-eyed needles (for sewing) – however, only allow the child to use sewing needles under adult supervision
- draws a person with head, body, mouth, eyes, nose and arms and legs.

Activity

Planned activities that make best use of the large muscle groups are ones that involve jumping, leaping and climbing. Encourage children to practise these skills by setting up a simple obstacle course. Try using tables to crawl under, boxes to jump over and a hoop to crawl through.

Inclusion point

Set up individual obstacle courses so that every child has a chance to succeed at their level of ability and, at the same time, is offered a bit of a challenge. Remember to adapt the activity so children with additional needs can participate.

EYFS

Practises some appropriate safety measures without direct supervision.

Adults can... Discuss with children why they get hot and encourage them to think about the effects of the environment, such as whether opening a window helps everybody to be cooler.

Balancing on one foot

Level 2: He can stand on one foot.

Level 3: Balance and coordination are improving rapidly.

Communication and language development

Key debate

'Theory of mind' is all about a child's belief about what is in the mind of another person. By the time they are five years of age, children are likely to be well on the way to developing theory of mind.

Observe children of this age playing together: listen/observe for evidence they are developing theory of mind. Note the words they use to describe other people's thoughts and feelings.

Inclusion point

Help children to associate particular words (or sounds) with people, activities and objects, possibly using visual prompts.

He/she:

➤ enjoys conversations with adults and children
➤ asks: 'What if?'
➤ asks: 'What does that mean?'
➤ loves to tell and make up jokes
➤ can pronounce most sounds of their heritage language
➤ shows interest in reading and writing
➤ can recognise their name in writing.

Using phone

Level 2: He shows interest in computer competence and will often surprise adults by the speed at which he learns.

Level 3: As he is growing up in the digital world, his expectations of technology are greatly increased.

Activity

Expressing how we feel, what we imagine and dream about, what we want to happen and what we don't like gets to the core of what it means to feel understood. Design an activity that helps a particular child express themself.

Inclusion point

When children find it hard to express themselves, adults need to find ways to make it easier. If you have a child who has communication challenges, try a range of activities to see which works best, for example puppets, flip cameras, photos, symbol cards, paint or other creative resources.

EYFS

Introduces a storyline or narrative into their play.

Adults can... Encourage language play, e.g. through stories such as 'Goldilocks and the Three Bears' and action songs that require intonation.

Intellectual development

He/she:

➤ may ask abstract questions, e.g. 'What if?'
➤ can say all or some of their personal details, e.g. address and age
➤ draws with more detail
➤ understands connection between time and events
➤ may act out scenes, either on their own or with others
➤ retells stories
➤ shows an in-depth knowledge of things that are of interest to them
➤ is able to give their attention to more than one thing at once.

Inclusion point

Braille or keyboards with enlarged keys can be helpful for children who are partially sighted. Voice-activated software and digital voice recorders can also be useful.

Using computer

Level 2: She shows an interest in reading.

Level 3: She understands the different purposes of words.

EYFS

Two-channelled attention – can listen and do for short spans.

Adults can... Give children opportunities both to speak and to listen, ensuring that the needs of children learning English as an additional language are met, so that they can participate fully.

AROUND SIX TO EIGHT YEARS

Video

Scan the QR code opposite to view a video demonstrating development for children around six to eight years.
You can also access this video at http://tinyurl.com/bkjvsrb

Personal, social and emotional development

Key debate

Researching in the 1960s and 1970s, Mia Kellmer Pringle discussed the importance of children feeling motivated (by themselves without others constantly motivating them) and how this all depended on the quality of their early social relationships.

Inclusion point

What practical ways could help a child who has lacked quality social interaction in their early years? Try to design a simple game that could meet their particular need.

He/she:

➤ is able to build strong friendships
➤ plays fairly, understanding rules
➤ has established hygiene and toileting routines

- is likely to play only in same-sex groups
- can be supportive and encouraging to others, particularly in games
- can consider others' wishes
- is better able to explain their feelings
- is becoming more self-aware, perhaps more critical of their own work
- can compare themselves to others
- can speak for themselves, e.g. at the doctor's.

Cutting apple

Level 2: He likes to help adults and can take part in food preparation with supervision.

Level 3: He can control his behaviour better and demonstrates a wide range of appropriate emotional responses.

Activity

Children at this age often enjoy gardening activities. Even if a garden isn't available, do try one of the following ideas: growing cress; making a window garden or cactus garden (you will need a large plant pot, pebbles, shingle compost, crocks and, of course, cacti). Why not consider an extension activity where you could encourage children to think about what plants need in order to grow?

Inclusion point

Children with autism can benefit emotionally from taking part in gardening activities, due to its therapeutic nature. With sensitive adult support, gardening can help to reduce anxiety levels and build self-esteem.

Physical development

Gross motor skills

He/she:

➤ moves with good balance and coordination
➤ can walk along a thin line with arms outstretched for balance
➤ can hop easily
➤ may ride a two-wheeled bike
➤ enjoys climbing frames and moves in a controlled way
➤ can catch a ball more easily
➤ has good control over their speed when running and can swerve to avoid a collision
➤ appears to be constantly 'on the go'
➤ can kick a ball three to six metres.

Fine motor skills

He/she:

➤ has well-developed pencil control and their grasp is similar to an adult's
➤ can build a straight tower
➤ draws with increasing detail.

> **Learning new skills**
>
> **Level 2:** He can sew if taught but needs a large needle.
>
> **Level 3:** He has improved hand–eye coordination, which opens up a world of possibility to try new skills.

Activity

Around this age, children often enjoy the challenge of trying out new skills. Try offering children sewing activities with a large needle, or simple cooking activities, such as making scones or pressing leaves – all great for helping to refine fine motor skills.

Inclusion point

Always be aware of children with high ability, to ensure that they too are constantly challenged to learn new skills.

Communication and language development

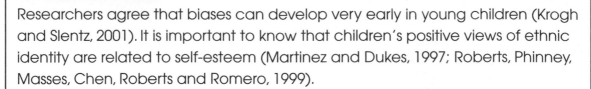
He/she:

➤ uses roughly four to seven words to make sentences
➤ uses 'could' and 'would'
➤ is using continual questioning less
➤ loves to talk
➤ can answer the phone in a mature and clear way
➤ may still have some difficulty pronouncing some sounds in the English language
➤ may speak more than one language – if this is the case, the degree of fluency in each language will vary
➤ tells more complex jokes
➤ may sometimes get mixed up with past/present tenses and singulars/ plurals.

Learning to tell the time

Level 2: Enjoys talking about things that happened yesterday and in the future and is beginning to understand how to tell the time.

Level 3: Understands the rules of turn-taking in conversation.

Activity

Children at this age are beginning to want to talk about more complex concepts such as how rain is formed. Why not make a simple weather vane? Then talk about the movement and direction of clouds. Other extension activities could include a whole project on weather and seasonal changes.

Intellectual development

Key debate

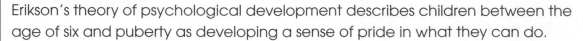

Erikson's theory of psychological development describes children between the age of six and puberty as developing a sense of pride in what they can do.

With this in mind, how can you help a child to develop a healthy sense of pride in self-chosen activities?

Inclusion point

If a child is experiencing low self-esteem and appears very critical of their achievements, how can you ensure that they begin to value themselves?

He/she:

➤ understands more abstract humour
➤ draws more sophisticatedly
➤ is developing literacy skills (reading and writing) and beginning to read independently between seven and nine years.

Activity

With help, children at this age can write a short script, which they can perform together. They will enjoy working out how the stage might look, building props and getting simple costumes together. Note how the children cooperate over a task. What strategies do they use?

Inclusion point

Be sure that all children can participate in getting the play ready – guide children to the part in the process they can best achieve and help them value contribution from their friends.

Measuring

Level 2: He asks more about how things work.

Level 3: Enjoys practical mathematics, such as measuring activities. Can count up to 100.

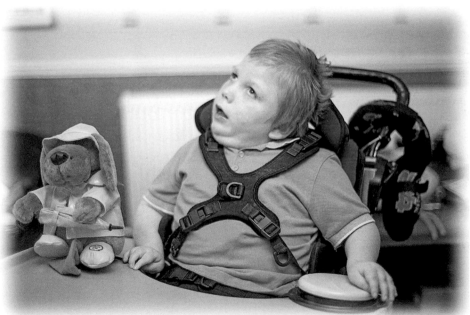

Activating toy

Level 2: He enjoys using a computer, operating digital equipment with increasing skill.

Level 3: He enjoys new digital challenges and understands cause and effect.

13 AROUND EIGHT TO TWELVE YEARS

Video

Scan the QR code opposite to view a video demonstrating development for children around eight to twelve years.
You can also access this video at http://tinyurl.com/a7pzk3x

Personal, social and emotional development

Key debate

Psychologists such as Bowlby, Freud, Erikson and Sroufe, working during the 20th century, all speak of the importance of early social and emotional experiences on later outcomes. In addition, policymakers have now recognised the importance of early intervention programmes.

Inclusion point

From your observations of children, how important do you think it is to support children in their relationships and in helping them handle their own emotions?

He/she:

➤ can be very concerned about what others think of them
➤ may enjoy belonging to clubs
➤ takes greater pride in their work

- can become quite bossy
- may place a lot of value on same-sex friendships
- may get embarrassed easily
- has an increased understanding of generosity.

Activity

At a time when children are beginning to truly relate to how others are feeling, the opportunities to reinforce care and sensitivity towards both humans and animals should be encouraged. Trips to farms and reptile centres can be a useful way to discuss care of creatures.

Expressing emotions

Level 2: She can relate better to other people's feelings.

Level 3: She is able to talk more about her own and others' emotions.

Physical development

Gross motor skills:

He/she:

➤ has a quicker reaction time
➤ may enjoy sports and energetic games
➤ has increased body strength and coordination.

Riding a bike

Level 2: He enjoys riding a bike, with impressive control.

Level 3: He has stronger muscle tone.

Fine motor skills:

He/she:

➤ has more control over their body, can write and draw with greater dexterity
➤ draws in a realistic way, may use depth and shading
➤ uses joined-up handwriting
➤ can draw three-dimensional pictures.

Activity

Dancing is a great way to get children moving and exercising. Children at this age often like to choreograph their moves. All they need is an audience!

Communication and language development

Key debate

Bruner (1996) discussed 'scaffolding' as a way that adults can help children develop their thinking. 'Scaffolding' describes the process of gradual withdrawal of adult support as a child begins to master a given task.

Describe the kind of language that an adult might use when helping a nine-year-old understand new mathematical concepts.

Inclusion point

Children with low self-esteem can benefit from activities being broken down into manageable chunks – allowing them to achieve success every step of the way.

He/she:

➤ may still like to talk a lot
➤ can write reasonably long pieces of work when motivated
➤ may express their ideas clearly
➤ can use and understand complex words and sentences
➤ reads and tell stories with increasing fluency
➤ is beginning to use reference materials online and books.

Playing an instrument

Level 2: She may display special talents in writing, art or music.

Level 3: A child with high ability who has her needs met will flourish emotionally and intellectually.

Activity

With such a desire to talk about new ideas, thoughts and feelings, it might be a good time to offer an inexpensive and easily operated video or flip camera. Children can make their own TV shows by first designing a storyboard and then shooting to the script. Just take them through it step by step. They might also want to make their own music video!

Inclusion point

This kind of activity is particularly suitable for children who find it difficult to express themselves or who are perhaps a little withdrawn.

Intellectual development

Key debate

Sir Ken Robinson, an internationally recognised leader in the development of education, creativity and innovation, argues the case for the arts in schools. He believes that schools must develop broader curricula.

What benefits do you think the arts offer children of this age?

Inclusion point

Children with learning difficulties benefit enormously from working with malleable materials such as clay and dough – activities that don't have a specified end result can be therapeutic and satisfying.

He/she:

➤ shows preference for particular activities/subjects
➤ may particularly enjoy learning new skills, for example measuring and weighing
➤ can read and write confidently
➤ enjoys being given responsibility
➤ has a strong sense of will and is beginning to assert this through argument
➤ communicates preferences and desires
➤ has a more developed understanding of abstract humour and humour preferences.

Activity

At this age, children are keen to find out how things work. Try offering activities that encourage curiosity, such as how light affects the growth of sugar crystals. Together, pour water and sugar into two jars. Tape a piece of string to each lid and let the strings drop into the jars. Then replace the lids. Place one in strong light and the other in the dark. During the next few weeks, children will be able to see the growth of sugar crystals on the string. Talk together about how the light affects the way the crystals grow.

14 AROUND 12 TO 16 YEARS

Video

Scan the QR code opposite to view a video demonstrating development for children around 12 to 16 years.
You can also access this video at http://tinyurl.com/bbacb9j

Personal, social and emotional development

Key debate

Kohlberg, researching from the 1950s to 1980s, identified six stages of moral reasoning. The stage called conventional morality is when children see others both as individuals and as members of a unit. According to Kohlberg, children at this stage are concerned about being accepted by others. This stage begins at around age ten but can last for the whole of life.

Carol Gilligan (1982) considered Kohlberg's research biased and limited because he used only males during his studies. Usefully, Urie Bronfenbrenner studied children and schools in different cultures. He was mindful that many ethnic, religious and social groups often have their own rules for moral behaviour.

What behaviour have you witnessed where children appear to be more concerned about being accepted by others and living up to their expectations? How does that influence their behaviour?

He/she:

➤ may be very self-conscious about their physical appearance
➤ is developing their own ideas and values, which may be different from those of their parents

- can become more disobedient, breaking rules and guidelines set by adults
- develops and recognises sexual identity/sexual preference
- prefers spending time with friends over family
- is often strongly influenced by peers
- may experience drastic mood swings
- can be highly introspective at times
- may feel under pressure with exams on the horizon.

Activity

At this age, children and teens feel a great need to find their identity. Activities that help them discover their unique self are those which tap into their strong interests. For example, they may wish to learn how to design clothes, sing, learn a new craft such as sewing, or develop a physical skill such as fencing. Adult interest and encouragement to persist at their interests will work wonders. They need to know they are not alone and that someone believes they can achieve through their talents.

Inclusion point

Belief in each child as unique and able is fundamental to caring and supporting every child regardless of their abilities or challenges. It is also important to acknowledge each child's emotional maturity level when choosing an activity.

Understanding others

Level 2: He is becoming more socially intelligent and better able to resolve conflict.

Level 3: He is better equipped to understand others' perspectives and feelings.

Physical development

Key debate

In the *British Journal of Sports Medicine*, 2006, an article on trends in physical activity and sedentary behaviour in adolescence by Naomi Henning Brodersen *et al.* discusses research in London schools. The results of this research showed that physical activity declines and sedentary behaviour becomes more common during adolescence. The researchers found that these effects are largely established by age 11–12 years, so they discussed the need to reverse these patterns in earlier childhood.

How can teenagers be encouraged to take part in more physical activities?

Inclusion point

Practitioners need to be continually alert for signs that an adolescent is being bullied or is isolated, and intervene.

Physical changes

Boys:

➤ growth of pubic and underarm hair
➤ voice deepens
➤ chest broadens
➤ may get chest hair
➤ muscles develop
➤ facial hair grows
➤ grow taller
➤ may get penile erections more frequently
➤ acne may appear
➤ start sweating more (sweat produced by the apocrine glands in the armpits and genital areas).

Girls:

➤ breasts develop
➤ fat develops on hips, thighs and buttocks

- grow taller
- pelvic bones grow
- curved body shape develops
- hips widen
- menstruation can begin at any time between the ages of 9 and 16, but will most commonly to start at 12 or 13
- acne may appear
- start sweating more (sweat produced by the apocrine glands in the armpits and genital areas).

Hanging out together

Level 2: Teens are coming to terms with their own physical changes.

Level 3: Hormonal changes can result in the need for greater reassurance from adults, although teens will rarely ask for the support they need.

Activity

At a time when adolescents are studying for exams or getting ready for exams, it is important to encourage activities to get them up and moving. Encourage them to make time for physical activities that capture their interest.

Inclusion point

Some adolescents prefer more solitary physical activities such as running, while others prefer cooperative games such as table tennis.

Communication and language development

He/she:

➤ may stop communicating respectfully or sensitively to parents
➤ may start to reply to parents in grunts or one-word answers
➤ often changes the way they speak and language will be heavily influenced by peers
➤ will probably choose to use fashionable language over grammatical correctness
➤ will have an improved understanding of language and grammar
➤ is likely to start communicating their own ideas and beliefs – however, ideas may not be thought through and this makes the communication staggered and inconsistent
➤ can communicate preference for school subjects and perhaps career choices.

Activity

Being social and keeping in touch with friends is a real driver at this age, alongside wondering if they fit in and are accepted by their peer group. You may want to use popular TV shows such as soaps to start discussions around these topics and to raise issues such as conflict with friends and how to resolve it.

Using technology

Level 2: May prefer to talk to peers rather than parents/carers.

Level 3: As hormones are changing, they may become reclusive in the home/family environment and only want to communicate with peers.

Intellectual development

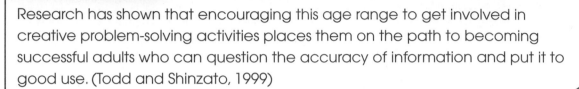

Key debate

Research has shown that encouraging this age range to get involved in creative problem-solving activities places them on the path to becoming successful adults who can question the accuracy of information and put it to good use. (Todd and Shinzato, 1999)

Inclusion point

Many people use self-talk to let off steam or to 'think out loud'. It is normal for teens with Down's syndrome to talk to themselves. This can be useful to know how they are feeling about a task and respond by offering materials to encourage further development.

He/she:

➤ has an increased reaction time
➤ can think abstractly.

Activity

There are several techniques that can support long-term memorising of facts and, with exams looming, it might be a good idea to investigate them together. Mind-mapping is a popular and effective way of taking notes that are memorable. In simple terms, it involves identifying central themes and using branches to represent connected concepts, words or ideas to relate them together.

Working for exams

Level 2: He may be highly skilled in specific areas.

Level 3: Can be very self-critical and needs encouragement from family and friends.

Reading news

Level 2: She is more globally and morally aware.

Level 3: She will question information given and the source of the information.

15 AROUND 16 TO 19 YEARS

Video

Scan the QR code opposite to view a video demonstrating development for children around 16 to 19 years.
You can also access this video at http://tinyurl.com/abmsu86

Personal, social and emotional development

Key debate

Davies and Furnham (1986) discussed how the adolescent can be critical of changes in their physical self. How much do you think young people are confronted by standards of beauty set in the media?

Inclusion point

Young people can be vulnerable to teasing and bullying by other young people if they are seen to be over- or underweight (Kloep and Hendry, 1999). Adults need to on the lookout for negative behaviour and its impact, and intervene as soon as possible.

He/she:

➤ will have developed their unique sense of humour
➤ may be more risk-taking
➤ has a greater understanding of themselves

- may have a more mature sense of self
- give greater focus to personal relationships with girlfriends/boyfriends
- may find that gaining a job/moving on to further education can occupy their minds and be a further pressure.

Teens going out

Level 2: Teenagers experience and enjoy a greater sense of independence.

Level 3: An improved ability to compromise lends itself to more positive relationships with others in the give and take of life.

Activity

Around this age, young people tend to feel strongly about areas that interest them, such as environmental or ecological concerns, or rights of particular groups. Whether or not you feel their views are justified, try to support their interests. Suggest that they express their thoughts in a visual format, such as a poster. Remember that everyone has a right to have an opinion and all views should be listened to.

Physical development

Key debate

Researchers agree that coming to terms with puberty is a huge adjustment for adolescents (Coleman and Hendry, 1990). Adolescents will all experience the same bodily changes but the rate at which that happens will vary. Some girls' menstruation starts earlier than others'.

How do you think adults can support teenagers through these changes?

Boys:

➤ brain development is continued
➤ advanced growth of secondary sex characteristics (e.g. facial and body hair)
➤ may have acne.

Girls:

➤ brain development is continued
➤ advanced growth of secondary sex characteristics (e.g. breasts)
➤ may have acne.

Teens listening to each other

Level 2: 95 per cent of adult height reached.

Level 3: Brain development: the prefrontal cortex is a little immature in teenagers as compared to adults.

Activity

Physically, teenagers may appear to be mature but they need plenty of support to value who they are while hormones are raging. One-to-one time becomes very important, as well as undertaking everyday activities together, such as tidying or preparation for daily routines. Sometimes adults simply need to listen to young people and to support and advise. Can you think of an occasion when you have not been listened to? If the role was reversed, how would you have managed the situation differently?

Communication and language

Key debate

A digital marketing agency, Click Consult, in 2012 found that 65 per cent of the 16- to 24-year-olds who were polled for the survey listed talking to their friends via Facebook and Twitter as their top leisure activity (quoted in the *Telegraph*, 21.7.12).

How might this shift in communication help or hinder the teenager's social life?

He/she:

➤ may draw away from intimate conversations with parents and families
➤ communicates very simply or bluntly with family, e.g. answering questions with just 'yes', no' or perhaps even just grunting
➤ may still adapt their language to that which is fashionable among peers
➤ begins to talk about what they want for their future in greater detail
➤ may communicate well-thought-out opinions and ideas about morals, religion and politics, that may or may not challenge those of their parents
➤ sometimes may not appear to be listening to adults during conversation.

Communication

Level 2: They may wish to communicate more consistently with peers than with family.

Level 3: They may still wish to communicate more through technology (e.g. texting), rather than face to face.

Activity

As communication can be troublesome at this age, find alternative ways for them to raise issues or concerns in an acceptable way – even if that isn't face to face. The arts can be a useful tool for communication. Try to discover the teen's preferred method of communication.

Intellectual development

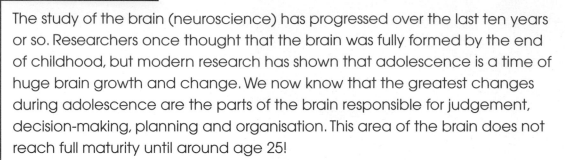

Key debate

The study of the brain (neuroscience) has progressed over the last ten years or so. Researchers once thought that the brain was fully formed by the end of childhood, but modern research has shown that adolescence is a time of huge brain growth and change. We now know that the greatest changes during adolescence are the parts of the brain responsible for judgement, decision-making, planning and organisation. This area of the brain does not reach full maturity until around age 25!

In the light of this information, how would you help a teenager to become more organised in their studies?

Inclusion point

Today, people who have Down's syndrome are living longer than in the early years of last century and if they are given greater opportunities to carry on learning, they can benefit from becoming lifelong learners.

He/she:

➤ has a greater ability to process abstract thoughts and concepts
➤ is equipped to make important decisions
➤ has developed work habits
➤ can set goals
➤ may be self-absorbed at times
➤ engages in speculative and independent thought.

Teens talking together

Level 2: They have an increased concern for the future.

Level 3: They are more open to the perspectives and views of others.

Activity

Set up a debate between groups of teens and encourage fair, respectful and equal debate. Note if a teen finds it particularly challenging to cope with conflict of opinion and set up extension activities to help them further.

16 OBSERVATIONS AND THE DEVELOPING CHILD

Children give us so many opportunities to learn about them – it's just a case of recognising those opportunities and using them as a basis for observations and assessments.

First, there are two key issues to remember:

➤ Keep everything about the child confidential at all times.
➤ Get permission before you start observing a child.

Several observations taken over a period of time can contribute much to parents and other professionals understanding the whole picture of how a child is developing.

Good record keeping

Good record keeping is all about keeping to the facts. Here are the four steps you will need to take:

1 **Before you start** observing you will need to write:
   ➤ the aim: why you are observing the child
   ➤ the date(s) and times of observation
   ➤ the age of the child
   ➤ a confidential way of identifying the child (e.g. Child B) – not the real name

➤ who provided the permission for you to observe
➤ where you did the observation
➤ who was around at the time (number of adults and children)
➤ how you did your observation (e.g. tick chart) and why you chose this way of doing it.

2 The next part is called the **Introduction**.
Describe what you are seeing right at the start: perhaps what has just happened, what equipment is around and any background information on the child (such as any absence from school). This all sets the scene for the next step.

3 **Observation** (what you see and hear)
You will already have chosen the method of recording (such as chart, checklist, written account), so this is where you complete it.

Two key issues to keep in mind:

➤ Don't ever write your opinion or judgement.
➤ Keep the child's name confidential.

4 **Evaluation**
This last step is about understanding and interpreting what you have recorded in step 2. This is where a book about child development comes in handy. You will need to think about the areas of development and skills of a child around this age and start to write about what you have learned through observation. The best way to start is to take an example of an area of development that you observed and rewrite it in this step. Then back up your observation with what you have read about in the book concerning a child of similar age.

Once you have done this, you are likely to have a good idea about how to help this child further. Perhaps you can suggest another activity that will strengthen the child's skills.

Building a tower sequence

Many children around 18–24 months (and older) enjoy building towers. The expression on their faces demonstrates the satisfaction achieved as the height increases.

17 CHILD DEVELOPMENT THEORIES

This chapter aims to provide you with a simple introduction to a selection of well-known theorists. It is important to build on these pages as you continue to learn more about the work of theorists.

The overview of their work is arranged alphabetically for simplicity and is not in order of priority.

Name	Dates	Location	Area of study	Main theories	Comments
Mary Ainsworth	Experimented in the 1960s	UK	Attachment	Experimented by measuring babies' responses to strangers when they were with their mothers, on their own and then reunited with their mothers. Used the term the 'sensitive mother' to describe mothers who respond promptly to the needs of their babies.	Worked with Bowlby (see below). Contributed to the debate about responsiveness and trust between mother and baby.
Chris Athey	Researched in the 1970s and beyond	UK	Schemas	Believes that a schema is a 'pattern of repeatable behaviour into which experiences are assimilated and that are gradually coordinated' (Athey, 1990: 37). Believes that there are two avenues of child development schemas: biological and socio-cultural aspects of development.	Her understanding of schemas has contributed to the work of early years workers during observation work and has served to inform curriculum planning.

(Continued)

Name	Dates	Location	Area of study	Main theories	Comments
Renee Baillargeon	Currently researching	Illinois	Cognitive development in infancy	Her team are exploring how infants make sense of the events they observe.	Conducted experiments with babies and found that they were well on the way to understanding object permanence earlier than Piaget thought.
Albert Bandura	Currently researching	Canada and USA	Many areas of psychology	Proposed a theory of child development, where children learn new behaviours from observing other people.	Unlike behavioural theorists, Bandura believed that a sense of pride, satisfaction and accomplishment could also lead to learning.
Dr John Bowlby	Researched from the 1950s to 1970s	UK	Attachment	Thought that: Early attachment is very important. Mother-and-baby relationships are very important. Babies need one central figure/carer. Children separated from their families in hospitals/ institutions went through stages of loss and grief.	Influenced by the research of James and Joyce Robertson. It is now thought that babies can develop relationships with more than one person. Bowlby's work led to the introduction of key workers and to changes in the treatment of children in hospitals and other institutions.

(Continued)

Urie Bronfenbrenner	1917–2005	Russia	The relationship between research and policy on child development	His theories concern ecological systems. Within this system he attempts to explain how everything in the child's environment affects the developing child.	
Tina Bruce	Currently researching	UK	Early childhood studies	Social learning theorist influenced by the work of Froebel (see below). Her theory on play includes 12 features: using first-hand experiences making up rules making props choosing play rehearsing the future pretending playing alone playing together having a personal agenda being deeply involved	Known for her ability to interweave theory and practice in creative ways. Discusses 'free-flow play' as the sort of play that children 'wallow in'; for example: freely chosen, pretending, role play, imagining or rehearsing, taking part in a 'personal play agenda'.

(Continued)

Name	Dates	Location	Area of study	Main theories	Comments
				trying out recent learning	
				coordinating ideas, feelings and relationships for free-flow play.	
Jerome Bruner	Researched from 1960s to 1990s	USA and UK	Social constructivism	Believed that adults can greatly help the development of children's thinking.	Developed Vygotsky's concept of the zone of proximal development.
				Believed that children learn by doing.	
				Identified enactive thinking, iconic thinking, symbolic thinking, and discussed 'scaffolding' as a way in which the adult can help develop a child's thinking.	
Noam Chomsky	Researched in the 1960s	USA	Language	Children are born with an innate capacity for language development. He called this a language acquisition device.	Contributed to the debate on language development.
				Human beings possess this predisposition to listen, talk and learn.	

Erik H. Erikson	Researched in the 1950s	UK	Personality development	Concerned with the superego and how society influences a child's development. He was influenced by Freud's work on the theory of personality.	Contributed to psychodynamic theories of development.
Sigmund Freud	Most productive period of psychoanalytical theory 1900–30, although some revision after this date	Austria and UK	Personality development	Founder of psychoanalytical theory and immensely influential in 20th-century theories of personality development. He believed that experiences in early childhood have a profound influence on personality and adult life. Freud identified different personality components as an 'id', 'ego' and a 'superego'.	His theories have always been regarded as controversial. He believed that his theories represented a major breakthrough in understanding development of personality.

(Continued)

(Continued)

Name	Dates	Location	Area of study	Main theories	Comments
Frederich Froebel	Experimented in the early years of the 19th century	Germany	How children learn	Expressed the importance of children having real experiences, including being physically active. Thought of schools as communities that included parents, whom he recognised as being the first educators of their children. Encouraged an appreciation of arts and craft and literature in addition to mathematical understanding. Thought that a child's best thinking is done when they are playing.	Has had a long-term influence on the education and care of young children.

Elinor Goldschmied	1910–2009	UK	Early childhood care and education	The pioneer of treasure baskets, heuristic play and the key person system. Her work influences theory and practice to this day.	Writing with Sonia Jackson, her work has influenced policymakers, managers, child care workers, social workers and students and parents.
Harry and Margret Harlow	Experimented in the 1960s and 1970s	USA	Attachment	Carried out experiments on monkeys, using isolating techniques and surrogate mothers, and concluded that contact and comfort are critical to emotional and social development. Proposed that there was a sensitive period of six months and if the monkeys were isolated for any longer they would never recover.	Bowlby (see above) drew conclusions concerning Harlow's experiments of maternal and social deprivation.

(Continued)

(Continued)

Name	Dates	Location	Area of study	Main theories	Comments
Lawrence Kolberg	Researched from 1950s to 1980s	USA	Moral reasoning	Extended Piaget's theories on moral reasoning. Identified six stages of moral reasoning in three levels: Level 1: pre-conventional morality Level 2: Conventional morality Level 3: Post-conventional morality.	Interested in the way children reason and justify their moral judgements. He does not tie his stages of moral reasoning to particular ages.
Konrad Lorenz	Experimented in the 1930s	Austria	Attachment and imprinting	Investigated the origins of baby animals' attachment to their carers and was the first to investigate imprinting – a very rapid form of attachment.	Pioneer in the science of ethology. Bowlby (see above) was influenced by the work of Lorenz.
Margaret McMillan	Researched from 1900 to 1932	UK	The development of nursery schools	Encouraged partnership with parents. Emphasised the importance of good nourishment and health.	Her work had an impact on school meals and medical services for children.

Loris Malaguzzi	1920–94	Italy	Educational experiences for children	Primary school teacher who went on to study psychology. Became the inspiration behind the educational experiences in Reggio Emilia.	Believed that creativity becomes more obvious when adults value the process rather than just the end result.
Jackie Marsh	Currently researching	UK	Early literacy and popular culture, media and new technologies	Exploring children's access to new technologies and their emergent digital literacy skills, knowledge and understanding, and is examining the way in which parents/carers and other family members support this engagement with media and technologies.	Theorists are beginning to examine the role of popular culture, media and new technologies in young children's early literacy development.
Cathy Nutbrown	Currently researching	UK	Early childhood education	Committed to finding ways of working 'with respect' with young children.	Her interest in inclusion extends to ways of developing inclusive practices where the voices of children, parents and practitioners are heard and their roles and perspectives valued.

(Continued)

(Continued)

Name	Dates	Location	Area of study	Main theories	Comments
Jean Piaget	Researched from 1920s to 1970s.	Switzerland	Constructivism, cognitive development, moral development, discovery learning, language development	Interested in the similarities between children. Showed that children actively construct their understanding of the world by interacting with it. Believed that logical thinking developed in steps: 0–2 years sensori-motor period; 2–7 years pre-operational period; 7–11 years concrete operations. Described mental structures and called them schemas. Developed 'the story-telling method' of investigation and drew conclusions about children's understanding of intentions and consequences.	He considered his work as a natural outgrowth of his biological studies. Thought that intelligence was not fixed at birth. Made a significant contribution to our understanding of cognitive development.

Mia Kellmer Pringle	Researched 1960s to 1970s	UK	Children's fundamental needs	Built on the work of Maslow (1962) and Isaacs (1968). Stressed the importance of intrinsic motivation based on the quality of a child's early social relationships.	First chief executive of the National Children's Bureau. Stressed the importance of a child's health and living conditions in relation to educational needs.
Sir Michael Rutter	Researched mainly from 1970s onwards	London and Isle of Wight	Nature/nurture debate Family break-up	Considered that there is a correlation between the amount of stress in the child's background and the likelihood of the child engaging in antisocial behaviour.	Concluded that early separation need not have lasting negative effects, but was less optimistic about the future of children who never made affectionate bonds.
B.F. Skinner	Researched in the 1930s	USA	Operant conditioning	Conducted experiments with stimuli and positive and negative reinforcements. Identified these responses as operant conditioning.	One of the leading figures in the development of behaviour modification. Chomsky (1960s) challenged Skinner's theories and carried out experiments which showed that language development is not a result of conditioning.

(Continued)

Name	Dates	Location	Area of study	Main theories	Comments
Barbara Tizard	Researched in the 1970s with Judith Rees and Jill Hodges	UK	Attachment	Showed that children are capable of forming close attachments to 'new mothers', even at a late age.	Contributed to the debate over the idea of a sensitive period. Showed that adoption can be a very satisfactory arrangement.
Colwyn Trevarthen	Researching currently	Scotland	Trained as a biologist and studied infancy research. Has written about brain development, infant communication and emotional health.	Showed how babies are ready and able to communicate.	Currently researching how rhythm and music impact babies.
Lev Vygotsky	Researched in the 1920s	Russia	Social constructivism	Believed that the child is an active constructor of knowledge and understanding. The main features of his theory concern the zone of proximal development. Discussed the importance of internalising social interactions and the importance of play.	Considered that the social and cultural context are crucial to a child's learning.

Donald Winnicott	Researched in the 1960s	UK	Attachment	Believed that play is essential to emotional and social development.
				Believed that the child's capacity to learn is directly related to the developmental stages of play.
				Identified comforters to which children become especially attached as being important transitional objects.

GLOSSARY

Adolescent: This term describes a child between the years of 13 and 19. 'Adolescence' is known as the transitional stage from childhood to adulthood.

Attachment theory: 'Attachment' is a description of the bond between a baby parent/carer and 'attachment theory' addresses how the parent's relationship with their child impacts development.

Autism: Autistic spectrum disorder (ASD) is a developmental disorder. The term Autistic Spectrum Disorder covers a wide range of conditions, including autism and Asperger's syndrome. It includes impairment in social interaction, communication difficulties and a preference for repetitive activities.

British Sign Language (BSL): BSL is a visual-gestural language (signs and gestures) with its own grammar. In March 2003, BSL was recognised by the Government as a language.

Cerebral palsy: This term covers a number of conditions where the brain doesn't work properly. It results in difficulties with movement and coordination.

Down's syndrome: Children with this syndrome have three copies of chromosome 21 rather than the usual two. Down's syndrome is a genetic condition that causes physical and intellectual impairments.

Early intervention: Early intervention in childhood describes the provision of services that can be remedial or preventive.

Empathy: Empathy is about understanding the feelings of others; it may be that you have experienced the same emotion yourself or that you can put yourself in their shoes. Empathy is not the same as sympathy.

Fine motor/manipulative skills: These concern the small movements of the body and use the muscles that enable, for example, the grasping of small objects, and the fastening of buttons.

Genetics: Genetics is the science of heredity: the passing down of traits from one generation to the next.

Gesture: Gestures are the use of movements to express thought and emotion.

Gross manipulative skills: These skills concern movements made by arms, legs, or the entire body. These skills involve the large muscles of the body that enable, for example, walking and kicking to develop.

Holistic development: This is an approach to child development that considers all the areas of development in a simultaneous manner.

Hormones: These can be considered to be chemical messengers which are released by a cell or a gland in one part of the body. These 'messages' affect cells in other parts of the organism.

Imagination: Imagination is the ability to form new mental images.

Inclusion: Inclusion is based upon the principle of ensuring that everyone has equal access to a service or activity, and that there are no barriers to an individual being 'included'.

Makaton: Makaton uses signs and symbols to help people to communicate and it supports spoken language. It is popular, as it allows children and adults to communicate straightaway using these signs and symbols.

Object permanence: This term relates to Piaget's well-known object permanence theory (understanding that objects exist even when they cannot be seen, heard, or touched).

Observations: These are detailed and focused notes/recordings of children's behaviour, actions and words over specified time frames.

Oxytocin: Oxytocin is a hormone. It also acts as a neurotransmitter in the brain. Researchers have now begun to investigate oxytocin's role in several behaviours, including strengthening our social relations and pair bonding.

Palmer grasp: This describes how an infant holds an item such as a crayon with the palm of their hand.

Parallel play: This kind of play describes how a child plays alongside another child but doesn't actually join in with their play yet.

Pincer grip: With this grip, a child uses only his thumb and index finger to manipulate small objects.

Picture Exchange Communication System (PECS): In this approach, pictures are used to develop communication skills.

Prone: This position is lying face down.

Puberty: Hormonal signals in the brain trigger puberty, which is the period in life when the body matures sexually and the reproductive organs can function.

Reflex: Reflexes are automatic responses to a stimulus.

Role play: Children can pretend during role play: they can assume different roles and personas and try out how it feels to be someone else. They will often use symbols to help 'pretend' and 'make believe'.

Scaffolding: This means to provide support to a child so they can master something that they are currently unable to master on their own. It helps the learner to figure out the task at hand on their own in the future.

Schema: A schema helps the brain to organise and interpret information in the world. It is an organised pattern of thought or behaviour.

Self esteem: Self-esteem represents judgements of one's own worth – positive or negative.

Signalong: This is a sign-supporting system based on British Sign Language. It was designed to help children and adults with communication difficulties.

Solitary play: This term describes play when a child explores materials or engages in activities all on their own.

Special educational needs: The term 'special educational needs' has a legal definition. The term refers to children who have learning difficulties or disabilities that make it harder for them to learn or access education than most children of the same age.

Spina bifida: Spina bifida means 'split spine' and is a condition whereby one or more of the vertebra in the backbone fail to form. The nerves in the spine may be unprotected, leading to damage of the central nervous system.

Visual impairment: The term 'visual impairment' refers to people with sight loss, covering a wide spectrum of different impairments.

REFERENCES AND FURTHER READING

Athey, C. (1990) *Extending Thought in Young Children*, London: Paul Chapman

Baillargeon, R. and DeVos, J. 'Object Permanence in Young Infants: Further Evidence.' First published online: 28 June 2008, *Child Development*, Volume 62, Issue 6

Bandura, A. (1977) *Social Learning Theory*. New York: General Learning Press

Bowlby, J. (1988) *A secure base, clinical applications of attachment theory*. London: Routledge

Bruner, J. (1966) *Studies in Cognitive Growth*. New York: John Wiley & Sons Inc

Bruner, J. (1996) *The culture of education*. Cambridge, MA: Harvard University Press

Chomsky, N. (1957) *Syntactic Structures*. London: Mouton

Davies, E. and Furnham, A. (1986) 'Body satisfaction in adolescent girls.' First published online: 12 July 2011, *British Journal of Medical Psychology*, Volume 59, Issue 3, pp. 279–287, September

DfES (1997–2003) 'The Effective Provision of Pre-School Education [EPPE] Project.' A Longitudinal Study funded by the DfES

Erikson, E.H. (1950) *Childhood and Society*. New York: Norton

Gilligan, C. (1982) *In a Different Voice: Psychological Theory and Women's Development*. Cambridge: Harvard University Press

Goldschmied, E. and Jackson, S. (1994) *People Under Three: young children in day care*. New York: Routledge

Hughes B. (2011) *Evolutionary Playwork*. Routledge: London

Malaguzzi, L. (1993) 'History, ideas and basic philosophy: an interview with Lella Gandini.' In Edwards, C., Gandini, L. and Forman, G. (eds) *The Hundred Languages of Children: The Reggio Emilia Approach – Advanced Reflections*. Second edn. Greenwich, CT: Ablex Publishing

Malaguzzi, L. (1993a) 'For an education based on relationships'. *Young Children*. November, 9–13

Moyles, J. (2001) 'Just for fun: the child as active learner and meaning maker.' In Collins, J., Insley, K. and Soler, J. (eds) *Developing Pedagogy: Researching Practice*, (pp. 4–10). London: Paul Chapman

Nutbrown, C. (1994) *Threads of Thinking: Young Children and the Role of Early Education*. Paul Chapman

Pavlov, I.P. (1927) *Conditioned Reflexes: An Investigation of the Physiological Activity of the Cerebral Cortex*. Translated and edited by G. V. Anrep. London: Oxford University Press

Piaget, J. (1936) *Origins of intelligence in the child*. London: Routledge & Kegan Paul

Piaget, J. (1945) *Play, dreams and imitation in childhood*. London: Heinemann

Piaget, J. (1957) *Construction of reality in the child*. London: Routledge & Kegan Paul

Schore, A.N. (2000) Plenary Address: 'Parent–infant communications and the neurobiology of emotional development.' In 'Proceedings of Head Starts Fifth National Research Conference, Developmental and contextual transitions of children and families. Implications for research, policy and practice', 49–73

Skinner, B.F. (1989) *The Origins of Cognitive Thought: Recent Issues in the Analysis of Behavior*. Merrill Publishing Company

Stephen, C., Dunlop, A.W. and Trevarthen, C. (2003) 'Meeting the Needs of Children from Birth to Three: Research Evidence and Implications for Out-of-Home Provision.' *Insight* 6: Edinburgh, Scottish Executive

Sturrock, G. and Else, P. (1998) 'The playground as therapeutic space: playwork as healing a paper for Play in a changing society.' 'Research, Design and Application', the IPA/USA Triennial conference, June

Todd, S.M. and Shinzato, S. (1999) 'Thinking for the future: Developing higher-level thinking and creativity for students in Japan – and elsewhere.' *Childhood Education*, 75, 342–345

Trevarthen, C. (1979) 'Communication and cooperation in early infancy. A description of primary intersubjectivity.' In M. Bullowa (ed.) *Before Speech: The Beginning of Human Communication*. London: Cambridge University Press

Watson, J.B. (1913) 'Psychology as the behaviorist views it.' *Psychological Review*, 20, pp. 158–177

Websites

www.early-education.org.uk
www.parentchannel.tv

INDEX